ISLAMIC ORNAMENTAL DESIGN

CLAUDE HUMBERT

1001 ornamental motifs

FABER AND FABER
London · Boston

Dédicace

Ce livre est dédié à tous les artisans anonymes et
modestes qui, durant des siècles, ont largement
contribué à l'éclosion et la perpétuation d'un art
riche, inventif et sensible.

Dedication

*For all the modest, anonymous artists who, over the
centuries, have contributed to the creation and
perpetuation of an art that is rich, inventive and full
of sensitivity.*

Widmung

Dieses Buch ist allen unbekannten und beschei-
denen Kunsthandwerkern gewidmet, die während
Jahrhunderten zum Werden und Fortbestehen
dieser reichen, erfindungsvollen und empfind-
samen Kunst beigetragen haben.

DESSINS *DRAWINGS* ZEICHNUNGEN
Cécile Caminada, Christiane Dussauge, Jean-Pierre
Meuer, Denise Mieville, Christine Morel, Martine
Rendu, Claude Rychner, Philippe Solms, Françoise
Vermot.
PHOTOGRAPHIES *PHOTOGRAPHS* FOTOGRAFIEN
Hélène Denizot, Jacques Henri, Claude Humbert.

*First published in 1980
by Faber and Faber Limited
3 Queen Square London WC1N 3AU
Printed in Austria*

*English translation by Alison Martin
German translation by Martin von Barnekow*

British Library Cataloguing in Publication Data

*Humbert, Claude
  Islamic ornamental design.
  1. Decoration and ornament, Islamic
  I. Title
  745.4'49'17671   NK1270*

  ISBN 0-571-11587-X

ISLAMIC
ORNAMENTAL
DESIGN

Table des matières   Contents   Inhaltsverzeichnis

Introduction

Le premier volume, «Ornamental design», a donné un aperçu général du motif ornemental et de son évolution à travers les civilisations de la préhistoire à nos jours. N'était-il pas important, par un premier complément, de faire une démarche plus spécifique pour tous ceux qui cherchent des références? Comme le premier volume, «Islamic ornamental design» est conçu pour une lecture essentiellement visuelle.

Le choix des motifs, couvrant l'espace géographique compris entre l'Inde et l'Andalousie, nous a été dicté par le fait que dans le cadre de cet espace il existe une constante: l'Islam.
En dépit de cette constante, les motifs réunis dans les pages qui suivent font la démonstration d'une grande variété. Ils sont répartis entre le VIIe siècle ap. J.-C. et la période contemporaine.

Sur une base de tracés très stricts, les motifs ornementaux sont les témoins vivants d'une grande liberté imaginative. De plus, ils ont pris la personnalité du pays qui leur est propre. Tandis que l'Occident dépouille et donne priorité à la géométrie et aux motifs stylisés, l'Orient pratique une expression plus descriptive et poétique.

Sur le plan graphique, nous nous sommes efforcés de respecter chaque technique en donnant ainsi aux motifs le caractère qui

Preface

This book is intended mainly as a visual guide. The designs cover the period from the seventh century A.D. to the present day and have been selected from an area extending from India to Andalucia, within which there exists a common denominator – Islam. Despite that common denominator, however, the designs that have been collected in the following pages show amazing variety.

While adhering to a very strict set of structural rules, these ornamental designs are nevertheless the surviving testimony of a truly creative imagination. In addition, they have assumed characteristics of the countries to which they belong. Damascus, the crossroads of the civilizations of east and west, may be taken as the starting point: to the east, the designs tend to be poetic and descriptive, with more plant and floral depiction; to the west, preference is given to geometric patterns and stylized motifs.
On the graphic side we have tried to be faithful to every technique, thereby reproducing the true character of the designs. They have been classified according to the principles set out in the Introduction.

The designs have been collected over several years in the course of many journeys and by research, in libraries and museums, into the secular and religious architecture of the Islamic countries. There

Einführung

Der erste Band »Ornamente« gab einen allgemeinen Überblick über Ornament-Motive und ihre Entwicklung von der Vorgeschichte bis heute. Was lag näher, als diesem Werk einen ersten Ergänzungsband folgen zu lassen, der die einzelnen Ornament-Motive noch genauer gegeneinander abgrenzt und der besonders für all jene gedacht ist, die nach speziellen Beispielen und Anregungen für eigene Arbeiten suchen. Wie der erste Band soll auch »Ornamente 2« vor allem durch die Vielzahl der Abbildungen informieren.

Die aus dem geographischen Raum von Indien bis Andalusien stammenden Motive haben einen gemeinsamen religiösen Hintergrund: den Islam. Trotzdem beweisen sie im einzelnen eine große Vielfalt.

Die gesammelten Motive umfassen die Zeitspanne vom 7. Jahrhundert n. Chr. bis zur Gegenwart. Auf einer strengen, vorgeschriebenen Form beruhend, sind sie lebendige Zeugnisse großer schöpferischer Freiheit. Von Damaskus, dem eigentlichen Kreuzungspunkt westlicher und östlicher Kulturen ausgehend, nehmen sie jedoch stets den Charakter des betreffenden Landes an. So finden wir im Orient vor allem aus poetischer Sicht dargestellte Blumen- und Pflanzenmotive, während der Westen klare Formen bevorzugt und Geometrie und Stilisierung den Vorrang gibt.

leur correspond. Leur classification est fonction des principes de base qui font l'objet de l'étude qui suit.

C'est au cours de nombreux voyages que ces motifs ont été réunis depuis plusieurs années, par une recherche dans les bibliothèques, les musées, sur l'architecture civile et religieuse des pays islamiques. La quantité impressionnante de ces documents nous a incité à faire un choix en fonction de leur variété, de leur époque, de leur technique et de leur nationalité.

Nous avons pris l'option d'une sorte d'inventaire tel qu'il soit un instrument de travail, source inépuisable de création quelle qu'en soit la forme.
L'analyse qui précède leur présentation permettra de mieux appréhender les motifs, également de mieux saisir, par une lecture avisée, toutes les possibilités subtiles qu'ils nous offrent.

is such an enormous quantity of material that a selection has had to be made, having regard to variety, period, technique and country of origin.

The designs are presented as an inventory – working models – which may be used as an inexhaustible source of creativity, no matter what the form employed may be. It is hoped that the analysis in the Introduction will give readers a clearer understanding of the designs and a better grasp of all the subtleties they reveal on close examination.

Die vorliegende Sammlung bemüht sich, jede Technik und ihre graphische Gestaltung zu respektieren und so die jeweiligen Eigenarten der Motive zu bewahren. Das hierbei angewandte Orientierungsprinzip entspricht der Einteilung nach Grundlinien, die sich durch das ganze Buch verfolgen lassen.

Die Motive wurden auf zahlreichen Reisen und während langjähriger Forschungen über profane und religiöse Architektur der islamischen Länder in Bibliotheken und Museen zusammengetragen. Aus der beeindruckenden Menge von Dokumenten mußte eine Auswahl getroffen werden, wobei die jeweiligen Eigenarten, Epoche, Technik und Landeszugehörigkeit zu berücksichtigen waren.

So entstand ein Werk, das als Arbeitshilfe und -anleitung und schier unerschöpfliche Quelle für eigene künstlerische Tätigkeit dienen kann.

Den Darstellungen geht eine Gliederung voraus, die ein besseres Verständnis der Motive ermöglicht und die Aufmerksamkeit auf die besonderen Feinheiten lenkt, die sie bieten.

1 Calligraphie signifiant l'invocation «O Dieu!» Par son graphisme souple et équilibré, elle démontre bien l'entière liberté dans l'invention.
2 Détail d'une écriture confrontée, contenant le nom de Dieu et du Prophète. On peut l'assimiler à la calligraphie pictographique.
3 Écriture koufique quadrangulaire dont la composition contient quatre fois les noms d'Ali et Mohammed. A noter, au centre de cette rigoureuse interprétation graphique, la sauvastika.
4 Écriture cursive andalouse (XIVᵉ siècle), ornementée de rinceaux. La technique délicate des carrés de céramique excisée n'enlève en rien la liberté dans le graphisme. Cette épigraphie exprime «Il n'y a de vainqueur que Dieu».

1 Calligraphy of the invocation 'O God!' The flowing yet well-balanced lines clearly indicate the total freedom of expression.
2 Detail of mirrored lettering comprising the names of God and the Prophet Muhammad. This may be classed with pictographic calligraphy.
3 Quadrangular Kufic script, repeating the names Ali and Muhammad four times. The sauvastika (right-handed solar cross) can be seen at the centre of this meticulous composition.
4 Andalucian cursive script (14th century), decorated with foliage. The delicate process of ceramic chasing does not check the artist's freedom of expression in any way. The inscription means, 'God is the only vanquisher.'

1 Kalligraphie, die Anrufung »O Gott!« bedeutend. Durch ihr schwungvolles und ausgeglichenes Schriftbild beweist sie die volle schöpferische Freiheit.
2 Detail eines spiegelbildlichen Schriftzugs, der den Namen Gottes und des Propheten enthält. Man kann ihn mit der bildlichen Kalligraphie vergleichen.
3 Viereckige Kufi-Schrift, deren Zusammensetzung viermal die Namen von Ali und Mohammed enthält. In der Mitte dieser strengen graphischen Ausführung steht das nach links gedrehte Hakenkreuz.
4 Andalusische Schrägschrift (14. Jh.), mit Ranken verziert. Die feine Technik der ausgeschnittenen Keramik mindert die Freiheit des Schriftbildes nicht. Die Inschrift bedeutet: »Es gibt keinen Sieger außer Gott«.

1

2

3

4

Approche du motif ornemental islamique:
Construction, structure et lecture

Introduction to Islamic Ornamental Design:
Construction, Structure and Interpretation

Das islamische Ornament-Motiv:
Aufbau, Struktur und Bedeutung

Les siècles qui suivirent l'hégire (an 622 du calendrier grégorien et début du calendrier hégirien) furent les témoins d'une explosion de conquêtes arabes. Cette guerre sainte donne à l'Islam sous les Abbassides (750-1258 ap. J.-C.) un espace géographique considérable d'est en ouest: Asie centrale, Ouzbékistan, Perse, Mésopotamie, Turquie orientale, Syrie, Arabie, Afrique du Nord, de l'Egypte au Maroc, Sicile et Italie du Sud, Espagne. Ce fut la plus grande expansion connue par les califats et les gouvernorats importants localisés.

Le passage de la civilisation arabe dans ces multiples régions a laissé des traces évidentes. Elles sont nées d'un mode de pensée et d'un mode de vie raffinés et subtils. Toutes les manifestations artistiques décoratives et ornementales puisent à leur source et s'intègrent avec harmonie dans leur environnement dont la lumière, l'eau, la verdure et la notion particulière du temps sont les éléments constitutifs principaux. Ceci est à mentionner, de même qu'il est important de parler des odeurs, notamment du cuir et du bois, et du toucher, à inclure également pour compléter heureusement la perception visuelle.

The centuries following the Hegira (622 of the Gregorian calendar) witnessed a succession of Arab conquests. The fiercely fought holy war enabled Islam, under the Abbasids (A.D. 750–1258), to spread to the east and to the west over a considerable area: to central Asia, Uzbekistan, Iran, Mesopotamia, eastern Turkey, Syria, Arabia, North Africa – from Egypt to Morocco – Sicily, southern Italy and Spain. The great expansion was achieved by the caliphates, the central and local Islamic ruling bodies.

As the Arabs passed through these different areas, they left clear traces of a civilization with a philosophy and a way of life that were both subtle and refined. All the decorative and ornamental art that was produced belongs to such a world, the main elements of it being light, water, greenness and a special conception of time. One should also mention the importance of the senses of smell, especially the smell of wood and leather, and of touch, a complement to visual perception.

Während der Jahrhunderte, die der Hedschra (Jahr 622 des Gregorianischen Kalenders, Beginn der Zeitrechnung des Islams) folgten, fand eine explosionsartige Ausdehnung der arabischen Eroberungen statt. Der mit Leidenschaft geführte Heilige Krieg brachte in der Abbasidenzeit (750–1258) die Besetzung eines beträchtlichen geographischen Raumes durch den Islam: Zentralasien, Usbekistan, Persien, Mesopotamien, östliche Türkei, Syrien, Arabien, Nordafrika von Ägypten bis Marokko, Sizilien und Süditalien sowie Spanien. Dies war die größte Ausdehnung der Kalifate, der wichtigen regionalen Herrschaftsbereiche.

Der Einbruch der arabischen Kultur hat in all diesen verschiedenen Gegenden sichtbare Spuren hinterlassen. Sie zeugen von einer kultivierten und verfeinerten Lebensart und Gedankenwelt. Alle künstlerischen, dekorativen und ornamentalen Erscheinungen schöpfen aus dieser Quelle und fügen sich harmonisch in eine Umgebung ein, deren wesentlichste Bestandteile das Wasser, die Pflanzen und ein eigener Zeitbegriff sind. Genauso wichtig ist es, die Sinne miteinzubeziehen, die die visuelle Wahrnehmung noch ergänzen, also z. B. Gerüche, besonders die des Leders und des Holzes, oder den Tastsinn.

5 Le carré est la base de construction géométrique polygonale la plus utilisée.
6 Interpénétration de deux carrés à 45°.
7 De cet agencement naissent les ornements géométriques polygonaux aux multiples de 4.
8 Le cercle, par sa division, couvre tous les ornements géométriques polygonaux construits sur les multiples de 3.
9, 10 L'ovale et l'ove sont des bases de structure pour les motifs ornementaux végétaux et floraux.

5 *The square is the most common structural unit in polygonal geometric designs.*
6 *Two squares overlapping at an angle of 45°.*
7 *This construction lends itself to the creation of polygonal geometric designs in multiples of four.*
8 *By reason of its divisibility, the circle is the basis for all polygonal geometric designs in multiples of three.*
9, 10 *The oval and the ovum are the structural bases for plant and floral ornamental designs.*

5 Das Quadrat ist das am häufigsten gebrauchte polygonale geometrische Grundelement.
6 »Überkreuzung« zweier um 45° gegeneinander verschobener Quadrate.
7 In dieser Anordnung entstehen die polygonalen geometrischen Ornamente im Vielfachen von 4.
8 Die Kreissegmente bilden alle polygonalen geometrischen Figuren im Vielfachen von 3.
9–10 Das Oval und die Eiform sind die Strukturgrundlagen für pflanzliche und florale Ornament-Motive.

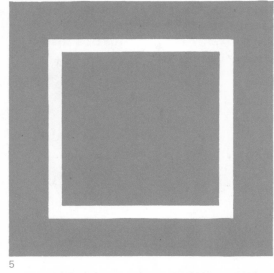

5

6

7

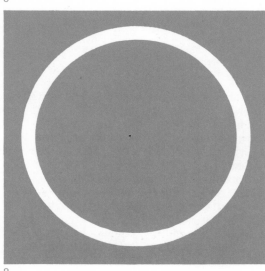

8

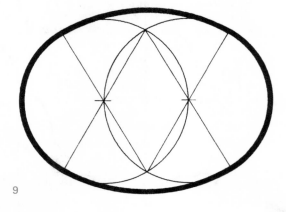

9

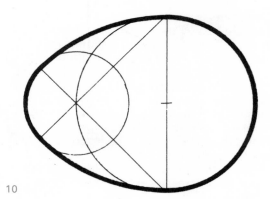

10

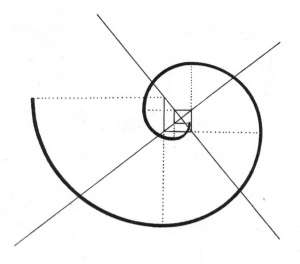

11

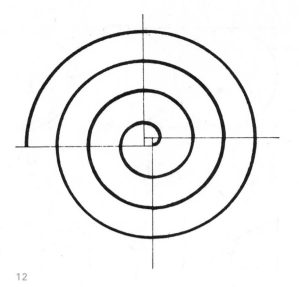

12

11, 12　La spirale complète la sinusoïde dans la structure des rinceaux.

11, 12　The spiral completes the sinusoid as a structural basis for foliage decoration.

11–12　Die Spirale ergänzt die Sinuskurve in der Struktur der Rankenornamente.

Si nous insistons sur ces constituantes d'une atmosphère remplie de calme et propice à la méditation, c'est parce que ces éléments ne peuvent être apparents dans les documents qui constituent ce répertoire de mille et un motifs ornementaux. L'option a été prise, en effet, dans la plupart des cas, d'isoler les motifs. Il n'en demeure pas moins que l'imagination d'un lieu tel que l'Alhambra de Grenade ou le palais d'Amber (pour ne prendre que les deux extrêmes géographiques) permet de restituer avec bonheur un contexte dont le rôle est important.

Le motif décoratif islamique, souvent fonctionnel à la base, se manifeste dans toutes les techniques: céramique utilitaire, céramique architecturale, azulejos et mosaïque de faïence, plâtre sculpté, pierre et marbre sculptés, marqueterie de marbre, bois sculpté assemblé ou peint, meubles, cuivre ciselé et gravé, textiles, tentes, etc. Telles sont les sources multiples exploitées pour ce répertoire.

Together these elements produce an atmosphere of calm, conducive to meditation. That has to be emphasized here; it will not be evident in the following pages, that form the repertory of 1,001 ornamental designs, because in most cases the motifs have been isolated. Nevertheless, the spirit of imaginative creation of places such as the Alhambra Palace at Granada and the Palace of Amber in India, to take two geographical extremes, fortunately makes it possible to reconstruct the context for the designs, which plays such an important role.

Examples of Islamic ornamental design, which is often basically a functional art, are to be found in all techniques: those of ceramics, tiles, tin-glazed earthenware azulejos and mosaics, stucco, carved stone and marble, marble inlay, carved, joined and painted wood, marquetry, furniture, chased and engraved copper, fabrics, hangings, and so on. This anthology gives specimens of each of them.

Jene Wesenszüge einer ruhigen, für Meditation günstigen Atmosphäre sollen hier besonders betont werden, denn sie ergeben sich nicht zwangsläufig aus den Grundelementen, die dieses Repertoire aus »Tausendundeinem« Ornament-Motiv bilden. In den meisten Fällen wurde so vorgegangen, die Motive isoliert zu betrachten.

Zweifellos wird aber die Vorstellung eines Ortes wie der Alhambra von Granada oder des Palastes von Amber (um nur zwei der geographischen Extreme zu nennen) dazu verhelfen, einen Kontext herzustellen, der zum Verständnis beiträgt.

Das islamische Schmuckmotiv, von der Basis her oft funktionell, erscheint in allen Techniken: Gebrauchskeramik, Baukeramik, Azulejos und Mosaiken aus Fayence, Stuck, behauener Stein und Marmor, Marmorinkrustationen, geschnitztes Holz, bemalt oder eingelegt, Möbel, ziseliertes und graviertes Kupfer, Stoffe, Behänge usw. Dies sind die mannigfaltigen Quellen des »Repertoires«.

13, 14 Sinusoïdes de construction simple. Les courbes plus ou moins serrées sont tracées par un brin.
15 Sinusoïde définissant une tresse à deux brins.
16 Tresse à deux brins parallèles.
17 Construction de la tresse à trois brins.

13, 14 Simple sinusoids. The wide or narrow curves are single-stranded here.
15 Sinusoid in the form of a double-stranded plait.
16 Plait with two parallel strands.
17 Triple-stranded plait.

13–14 Sinuskurven einfacher Art. Die mehr oder weniger engen Kurven werden in einem Strich gezogen.
15 Sinuskurve, die einen Zopf aus zwei Strängen bestimmt.
16 Zopf aus zwei gleichlaufenden Strängen.
17 Aufbau des dreifachen Zopfes.

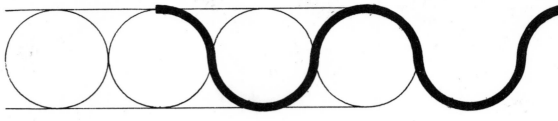

13

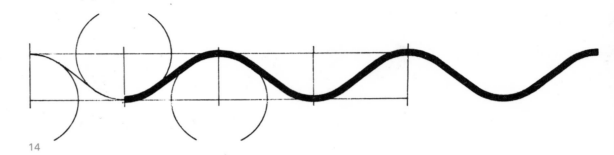

14

15

16

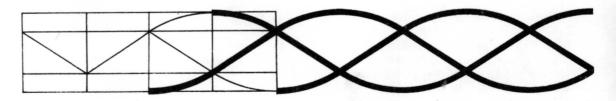

17

18

19

18, 19   Application simple de la sinusoïde (Fig. 13 et 14) dont le tracé devient structure du végétal qui l'habille.

18, 19   *Sinusoid (see Figs. 13 and 14) applied in a simple design, where it provides the structure of the foliage placed around it.*

18–19   Einfache Anwendung der Sinuskurve (Fig. 13 und 14). Der Kurvenstrich bildet die Grundstruktur der Pflanze, die ihn umgibt.

Il est à noter que le motif ornemental islamique, le plus souvent farci de détails et très fouillé dans son expression graphique, s'incorpore toujours avec bonheur et équilibre à un ensemble. Au fur et à mesure des conquêtes il s'est affirmé en marquant sa spécificité au lieu géographique, sans renier pour autant ses origines.

L'écriture, calligraphie ou épigraphie, est le témoin d'une civilisation. Non seulement les idées et les faits qu'elle transcrit et communique définissent un contenu, mais le graphisme ou tracé détermine le contenant. Ce dernier permet une analyse analogue à une analyse graphologique. Les quelques exemples en regard de ce texte (Fig. 1 à 4) sous-entendent beaucoup d'intelligence, d'invention, de rigueur et de totale liberté. Le plus étonnant, sans aucun doute et en confrontation avec certaines écritures occidentales, c'est la définition de l'attitude intérieure de l'artiste face à l'écriture, calligraphie ou épigraphie. La main qui trace est bien le prolongement de la pensée.

Although Islamic ornamental designs are often packed with elaborately drawn details, they always blend into a well-balanced whole. As the conquests proceeded, so the art established itself, taking on special forms from each area, yet never losing its original characteristics.

Writing, calligraphy and epigraphy are the testimony of a civilization. Not only do the ideas and deeds transcribed and communicated provide content, but the writing and the written page themselves constitute a form that can be analysed graphologically. The few examples relevant here (Figs. 1 to 4) suggest remarkable intelligence, inventiveness, precision and complete freedom of expression. The qualities of Arab civilization are indeed extremely varied.

Es ist bemerkenswert, daß das islamische Ornament-Motiv, das meist zahlreiche Details aufweist und sehr genau in seiner graphischen Ausführung ist, sich immer in gekonnter und ausgeglichener Weise in das ganze Werk einfügt. Es hat sich während der fortschreitenden Eroberungen dadurch behauptet, daß es seine Eigenheiten dem geographischen Charakter anpaßte, ohne seine Ursprünge zu verleugnen. Die Schrift, ob Kalligraphie oder Inschriftendekor, ist Zeuge und Ausdruck einer Kultur. So vermitteln die übertragenen und festgehaltenen Gedanken und Tatsachen nicht nur eine Aussage, sondern es bestimmt gleichzeitig die graphische Gestaltung und Linienführung die Form. Letztere erlaubt eine Analyse, die der graphologischen Analyse ähnlich ist. Die hier gezeigten Beispiele (Fig. 1 bis 4) zeugen von Intelligenz, Erfindungsgabe, Genauigkeit und völliger Freiheit. Beim Vergleich mit einigen westlichen Schriftarten ist das Erstaunlichste sicher die zum Ausdruck gebrachte innere Einstellung des Künstlers gegenüber der Schrift, sei sie Kalligraphie oder Inschriftendekor. Die zeichnende Hand ist die »Verlängerung« des Gedankens.

20 Mosaïque romaine. Réseau de cercles entrelacés dont l'agencement par 6 définit un hexagone en leur centre.

21 Cette ornementation arabe, dont le réseau est identique à celui de la figure 20, démontre toute l'invention qu'une lecture approfondie permet de déceler, notamment les entrelacs multiples et subtils, la structuration des sauvastikas et le rythme de répartition des hexagones.

22 Mosaïque romaine. Les carrés entrelacés définissant des étoiles à huit branches n'ont aucune relation avec les octogones qui occupent les espaces intermédiaires.

23 Bien que basée sur la même construction que le motif ornemental tracé en figure 22, cette ornementation arabe structure le motif en fonction de l'octogone.

20 *Roman mosaic. Tracery of circles interlaced in sixes, creating a hexagon at the centre of each.*

21 *The tracery of this Islamic design is identical with that of Fig. 20. Close examination reveals the great inventiveness of such a design, especially the numerous intricate patterns of interlacing, the structuring of the sauvastikas and the placing of the hexagons.*

22 *Roman mosaic. The pattern of interlaced squares forming eight-point stars is separate from the pattern of octagons formed by the intermediary spaces.*

23 *Although this Islamic design is based on the same construction as that shown in Fig. 22, the pattern here is related to the octagon.*

20 Römisches Mosaik. Netz aus verflochtenen Kreisen, deren Sechseranordnung in der Mitte je ein Sechseck entstehen läßt.

21 Dieses arabische Ornament (das Netz ist identisch mit dem von Figur 20) zeugt von großer Erfindungsgabe, wie man durch genaue Beobachtung erkennen kann. Besonders zu beachten sind das feine Flechtwerk, die Strukturierung der Hakenkreuze und der besondere Rhythmus in der Anordnung der Sechsecke.

22 Römisches Mosaik. Die verflochtenen Quadrate bilden Sterne mit acht Spitzen; sie sind unabhängig von den Achtecken der Zwischenräume.

23 Dieses arabische Ornament stellt ein Motiv in Form eines Achtecks in besonderer Weise heraus, obwohl es auf der gleichen Konstruktion gründet wie jenes von Figur 22.

20

21

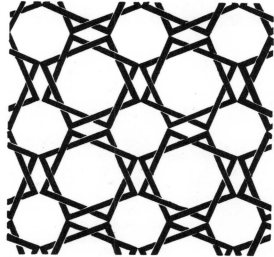
22

23

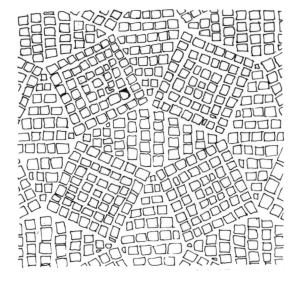

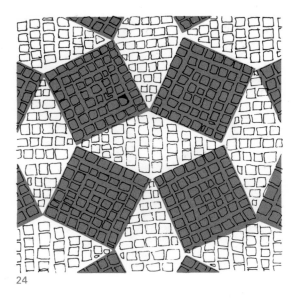

24

24 Mosaïque romaine. La pose des éléments de mosaïque monochrome définit un rythme de carrés et de losanges.
25 L'ornement arabe polychrome reprend ces rythmes qui varient suivant l'angle sous lequel on les regarde. Une lecture attentive nous permet également de les découvrir en trois dimensions.

24 *Roman monochrome mosaic, the pieces of which are arranged to form a pattern of squares and diamonds.*
25 *This Islamic polychrome design repeats the same patterns, which vary according to the angle from which they are viewed. A three-dimensional interpretation is also possible.*

24 Römisches Mosaik. Die Verteilung der einfarbigen Mosaikelemente bestimmt den Rhythmus von Quadraten und Rhomben.
25 Das mehrfarbige arabische Ornament nimmt diese Rhythmen wieder auf, die sich je nach dem Winkel, aus dem man sie betrachtet, ändern. Durch aufmerksame Beobachtung entdeckt man sie sogar in drei Dimensionen.

25

D'autre part, la technique utilisée ne semble en rien enrayer la spontanéité du tracé de l'écriture. Preuve en soit la céramique excisée dont les médersas du XIVe siècle conservent encore de très beaux témoignages.
Cette technique consiste à enlever (sur des carrés de terre émaillés noir), au marteau aiguisé, tout l'émail autour des lettres et des rinceaux qui les ornent (Fig. 4). Les creux ainsi obtenus sont remplis de plâtre mélangé à de la chaux. L'écriture et les ornements qui l'accompagnent se détachent ainsi en noir sur blanc. Les raccords constitués par la juxtaposition des carrés sont parfaits, en dépit de la finesse du tracé ornemental.

Undoubtedly the most surprising feature— in total contrast to certain Western scripts – is the artist's personal attitude to his craft, whether it is calligraphy or epigraphy: the hand that writes is an extension of the mind. Moreover, the technique used does not seem to check in any way the spontaneity of the written line, as can be seen in the beautiful ceramic chasing of the fourteenth-century madrasahs (Muslim schools). This technique consists of removing with a pointed hammer all the glazing around the letters and decorative foliage on black-glazed earthenware tiles (Fig. 4). The resulting grooves are filled with a mixture of plaster and lime so that the decorated characters stand out in black and white. When the tiles are fitted together the lines of the design join perfectly, notwithstanding the fineness of the incision.

Andererseits scheint die angewandte Technik nicht im geringsten die Ursprünglichkeit der Schriftzüge zu hemmen. Beweis hierfür ist die »ausgeschnittene« Keramik, von der die Medresen des 14. Jahrhunderts noch sehr schöne Zeugnisse bewahren.
Diese Technik besteht darin, auf Rechtecken aus schwarz glasiertem Ton mit einem spitzen Hammer die Glasur rund um die Buchstaben und das Laubwerk zu entfernen (Fig. 4). Die so erhaltenen Hohlräume werden mit einer Mischung aus Gips und Kalk ausgefüllt. Schrift und Ornamente heben sich somit Schwarz auf Weiß ab. Trotz der Feinheit der ornamentalen Zeichnungen erfolgen die Übergänge bei den nebeneinanderliegenden Rechtecken gleichsam nahtlos.

26

27

26 Cette disposition réticulée d'éléments simples, construits sur une base de carrés, définit un réseau traditionnel utilisé dans les sols en céramique.

27 Motifs dérivés des étoiles octogonales. Les formes qui relient les étoiles sont identiques et s'emboîtent par quatre sur la base d'une svastika. Cette ornementation est généralement réalisée en mosaïque de faïence polychrome.

26 *This repeating pattern, constructed on a base of squares, shows a traditional design used for ceramic floors.*

27 *Motifs created out of octagonal stars. The figures that link the stars together are identical in shape and join in fours to form swastikas. This design is usually carried out in a mosaic of polychrome (tin-glazed) earthenware.*

26 Diese netzartige Anordnung einfacher Elemente auf einer Grundlage von Rechtecken ergibt ein traditionelles Geflecht, das besonders bei Keramikböden Anwendung findet.

27 Aus achteckigen Sternen abgeleitete Motive. Die Formen, welche die Sterne verbinden, sind identisch und fügen sich zu viert ineinander nach dem Muster eines nach rechts gedrehten Hakenkreuzes. Dieses Ornament wird häufig als Mosaik in mehrfarbiger Fayence ausgeführt.

N'oublions pas que l'écriture arabe est née avant l'Islam. Une inscription trilingue (grecque, syriaque et arabe) de Zabad, près d'Alep, est datée de 512-513 ap. J.-C. Une seconde, bilingue (grecque et arabe), découverte à Harran, date de 568 ap. J.-C. D'autre part, l'alphabet arabe est utilisé par des peuples musulmans parlant des langues autres que l'arabe et parfois même non sémitiques.
L'écriture arabe reste cependant, dans le monde musulman, le véhicule de la langue classique comprise par tous les lettrés.

Il était important de consacrer quelques lignes à l'écriture, car elle fait partie intégrante de la décoration arabe. C'est un ornement en soi qui vient tout naturellement s'incorporer aux autres.

It is important to consider briefly here this script that forms an integral part of Arab design. Ornamental in itself, it quite naturally comes to be incorporated into other ornaments. Arabic script came into existence before Islam. In Zabad, near Aleppo, there is a trilingual inscription (Greek, Syrian and Arabic) that has been dated to A.D. 512 or 513, and a bilingual inscription (Greek, Arabic) dating from A.D. 568 has been discovered at Harran. Moreover, the Arabic alphabet is used by Muslim peoples who speak languages other than Arabic, and sometimes even by non-Semitic peoples. Arabic script, however, remains the vehicle of the classical languages and is used by all educated people in the Muslim world.

Man darf nicht vergessen, daß die arabische Schrift schon vor dem Islam bestand. Eine dreisprachige Inschrift (griechisch, altsyrisch und arabisch) aus Zabad, in der Nähe von Aleppo, datiert aus den Jahren 512–513 n. Chr. Eine weitere, in Harran entdeckte zweisprachige (griechisch und arabisch), stammt von 568 n. Chr. Darüber hinaus verwenden auch muslimische Völker, die nicht das Arabische, ja manchmal sogar nichtsemitische Sprachen gebrauchen, das arabische Alphabet.
Die arabische Schrift bleibt deshalb in der mohammedanischen Welt die von allen Gebildeten verstandene Ausdrucksform der klassischen Sprache.

Es war notwendig, der Schrift einige Zeilen zu widmen, weil sie einen geradezu wesentlichen Bestandteil der arabischen Dekoration darstellt; sie ist Ornament an sich, das sich auf natürliche Weise mit anderen Ornamenten vereint.

28

29

28 Le motif ornemental est, ici, unique. Ces feuilles de figuier stylisées s'ajustent les unes aux autres, face à face ou dos à dos, selon un réseau défini par les verticales (motifs noirs) et les horizontales (motifs blancs). Motif traditionnel à variantes, couramment exécuté en mosaïque de faïence polychrome.

29 Les formes semblables à celles de la figure 28 sont définies par des entrelacs. Cette adaptation modifie le visage du réseau qui devient linéaire. C'est ainsi qu'apparaissent, en toute évidence, les svastikas et les sauvastikas.

28 *Design composed of a single motif. The stylized fig leaves fit together, face to face or back to back, to form a pattern of verticals (black figures) and horizontals (white figures). This is a traditional design with variations, usually carried out in a mosaic of polychrome (tin-glazed) earthenware.*

29 *Here the shapes, similar to those in Fig. 28, are formed by the interlacing. This adaptation modifies the pattern, which becomes linear, thereby creating swastikas and sauvastikas, both clearly in evidence.*

28 Dieses Ornament-Motiv steht hier allein: es stoßen jeweils die Vorder- oder Rückseiten der stilisierten Feigenblätter aneinander, einem Muster folgend, das durch die Senkrechten (schwarze Motive) und die Waagrechten (weiße Motive) bestimmt wird. — Traditionelles Motiv mit Varianten, meist als Mosaik in mehrfarbiger Fayence ausgeführt.

29 Die der Figur 28 ähnlichen Formen werden vom Flechtwerk bestimmt. Diese Anpassung gibt dem Geflecht ein lineares Aussehen. Auf diese Weise werden die nach rechts und links gedrehten Hakenkreuze sichtbar.

Si l'on examine, dans l'espace géographique que nous avons délibérément choisi, toutes les manifestations d'art décoratif et ornemental arabe, on peut discerner deux types bien distincts: la décoration polygonale dont la singularité est l'utilisation avisée et savante de la géométrie, et la décoration végétale et fleurie (terme utilisé par Collin) qui, contrairement à la première, cherche son inspiration dans le monde qui nous entoure.

Ces deux types de décoration sont définis par deux écoles. L'école du Maghreb (Maroc, Algérie, Tunisie) est très représentative de l'Occident. Il semble que les artistes ont puisé en eux les sources d'inspiration pour les extérioriser. Il s'agit donc de communiquer à un monde extérieur toutes les richesses d'un monde intérieur.
Tout naturellement, la géométrie se prête à ce jeu dont les règles sont bien définies.

From an examination of all the forms of decorative and ornamental Islamic art, two quite distinct types emerge: polygonal ornamentation, characterized by a skilled and critical use of geometry; and plant and floral ornamentation (terms used by Collin), which, in contrast to polygonal design, are inspired by the natural world. These two types of design belong to two different schools.

The Maghreb School (Morocco, Algeria, Tunisia) is representative of the west. The artists seem to have drawn from sources of inspiration within themselves and to have expressed their art by communicating all the richness of this inner world to the outer world. Geometry lends itself easily to the process, which has very precise rules; however, such strict rules do not act as a constraint. On the contrary, they facilitate and give greater emphasis to artistic invention and expression. That becomes clear in the process of decipher-

Untersucht man innerhalb des gewählten geographischen Raumes alle Erscheinungsformen der arabischen Ornament- und Dekorationskunst, dann erkennt man zwei unterschiedliche Typen: die polygonalen Verzierungen, deren Eigentümlichkeit die umsichtige und kunstvolle Anwendung der Geometrie ist, und die pflanzlichen und floralen (von Collin gebrauchter Begriff) Verzierungen, die, im Gegensatz zu den ersten, ihre Anregungen in der belebten Welt suchen.

Diese beiden Dekorationstypen werden durch zwei Schulen bestimmt. Die Schule des Maghreb (Marokko, Algerien, Tunesien) ist charakteristisch für den Westen. Die Künstler scheinen aus einer inneren Quelle zu schöpfen, und es geht ihnen darum, die Reichtümer der inneren Welt einer äußeren Welt mitzuteilen.
Für dieses Spiel mit klaren Regeln eignet sich die Geometrie ganz besonders. Dennoch ist die Strenge dieser Regeln

30 Sans hésitation, cette forme envelop-
pante se lit de l'intérieur, en blanc.
31 La moitié de la forme, définie en figure
30, nous permet d'en aborder la lecture
par l'extérieur, en noir.
32 La contrepartie est définie par une lecture
de la forme extérieure identique à celle
de la forme intérieure. Motif traditionnel
de merlons et de charafats.
33 Réseau de contreparties sur le rythme
vertical et horizontal.

30 *This enclosed form is easily visible in the
white interior.*
31 *Half the design shown in Fig. 30 from a
changed viewpoint: the black exterior.*
32 *Reciprocal pattern, where the outer
shape is identical with the inner one. Traditional design of merlons and crenels.*
33 *Reciprocal pattern of identical counter-
parts on vertical and horizontal axes.*

30 Diese umschließende Form läßt sich ganz
klar vom Inneren – in Weiß – heraus erkennen.
31 Die eine Hälfte der Form von Figur 20
erlaubt, sie von außen – in Schwarz – zu
betrachten.
32 Beim Betrachten der gegengleichen
Stücke läßt sich die Identität der äußeren
Form mit der inneren erkennen. – Traditionelles Motiv der Zinnen und *charafats.*
33 Geflecht aus gegengleichen Elementen in
senkrechtem und waagrechtem Rhythmus.

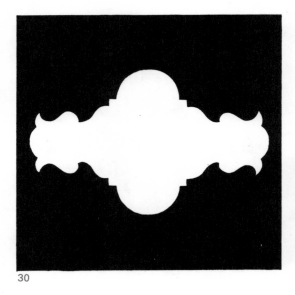

30

31

32

33

34

34 Répartition d'osselets en contrepartie. Motif d'influence romaine.
35 Répétition du nom d'Allah en écriture koufique quadrangulaire. La contrepartie en permet une double lecture. En noir sur fond blanc et, en imprimant au texte une rotation de 180°, en blanc sur fond noir.

34 Reciprocal pattern of knucklebones. Roman influence.
35 Repetition of the word Allah in quadrangular Kufic script. Because of the reciprocal arrangement, the design can be read in two ways: in black, on a white background and, turning the text upside-down, in white on a black background.

34 Verteilung von »Knöchelchen« als Gegenstücke. – Motiv mit römischem Einfluß.
35 Wiederholung des Namens Allah in rechteckiger Kufi-Schrift. Das Gegenstück ermöglicht eine doppelte Auslegung: schwarz auf weißem Grund oder, wenn man den Text um 180° dreht, weiß auf schwarzem Grund.

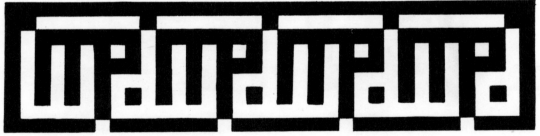

35

Néanmoins, la rigueur de ces dernières n'est pas contraignante. Elle favorise au contraire l'invention graphique et donne à l'expression plus de force. Ceci devient évident dans la recherche de lecture d'une ornementation géométrique polygonale lorsque notre esprit devient vide de toute autre pensée et préoccupation. Ce phé-

ing a polygonal geometric design: all other thoughts and preoccupations are driven from the mind. It can even induce a physical state of abstraction. Although geometry is of prime importance in the Maghreb School, plant forms are still to be found, even if they are elaborately stylized (Figs. 51, 52 and 62). These designs are

nicht zwingend. Im Gegenteil, sie begünstigt die graphische Erfindungsgabe und die Kraft des Ausdrucks. Die Wirkung auf den Betrachter eines polygonalen geometrischen Ornamentes kann so sein, daß er sich in einen Zustand geistiger Abwesenheit, ein Freisein von Denken und Handeln, versetzt sieht.

36 L'agencement de motifs ornementaux forme un réseau. Celui-ci peut se définir en isolant une structure dont la répétition détermine l'ornementation de la surface dans sa totalité.

37 Structure isolée du réseau défini en figure 36.

36 *This arrangement of ornamental motifs forms a pattern that can be analysed by isolating one figure which, when repeated, forms the whole design.*

37 *Structural element from the pattern shown in Fig. 36.*

36 Die verschiedenartige Anordnung eines einzigen Motivs bildet ein Geflecht; auch hier läßt das Prinzip der Wiederholung die Ornamentik der ganzen Fläche entstehen.

37 Isolierte Struktur aus dem in Figur 36 gezeigten Geflecht.

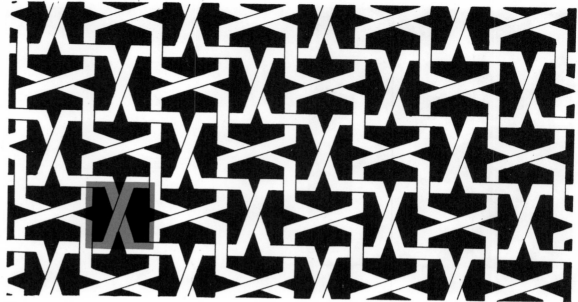

36

37

nomène va jusqu'à provoquer en nous un état physique d'absence.

Il faut noter cependant que si dans l'école du Maghreb la géométrie prime, le végétal est néanmoins apparent, dans une optique de stylisation très poussée (Fig. 51, 52 et 62). C'est la technique du plâtre sculpté (geps) qui en est le support dans la majorité des cas.

Par contre, la décoration fleurie réservée aux bois peints (zouacs) est d'une rare présence. Elle se manifeste, au Maghreb, avec une influence persane évidente.

carried out in stucco (gypsum) in the majority of cases. Floral decoration, on the other hand, which is limited to paintings on wood (zouacs), is uncommon, and when it does appear in the Maghreb a clear Persian influence can be seen.

Obwohl die Geometrie in der Schule des Maghreb vorherrschend ist, erscheint auch das pflanzliche Element in einer hochgradig stilisierten Weise (Fig. 51, 52 und 62). In den meisten Fällen ist es in geschnittenem Stuck (Gips) ausgeführt. Dagegen ist die auf das bemalte Holz (zouacs) beschränkte florale Verzierung sehr selten. Sie zeigt im Maghreb einen deutlichen persischen Einfluß.

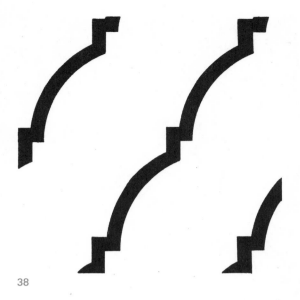

38

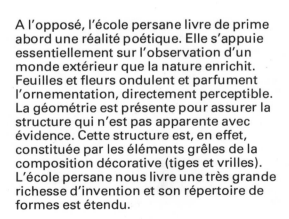

39

40

38 Pour cette lecture possible du réseau de la figure 40, la dénomination de réseau losangique lui a été attribuée.
39 Le motif ornemental défini par les intersections des obliques entrelacées, permet une autre lecture du réseau.
40 Réseau losangique, ornement courant des minarets rectangulaires.

38 This interpretation of the pattern shown in Fig. 40 is termed diamond tracery.
39 The motif formed by the intersection of the oblique lines provides another possible interpretation of this pattern.
40 Diamond tracery, commonly used on rectangular minarets.

38 Diese Struktur wurde als mögliche Lesart des Geflechts in Figur 40 »rautenartiges Geflecht« genannt.
39 Das Ornament-Motiv, das durch die Kreuzung von verflochtenen Schrägen entsteht, erlaubt eine andere Auslegung des Geflechts.
40 Rautenartiges Geflecht.– Übliches Ornament der rechteckigen Minarette.

A l'opposé, l'école persane livre de prime abord une réalité poétique. Elle s'appuie essentiellement sur l'observation d'un monde extérieur que la nature enrichit. Feuilles et fleurs ondulent et parfument l'ornementation, directement perceptible. La géométrie est présente pour assurer la structure qui n'est pas apparente avec évidence. Cette structure est, en effet, constituée par les éléments grêles de la composition décorative (tiges et vrilles). L'école persane nous livre une très grande richesse d'invention et son répertoire de formes est étendu.

In contrast, the Persian School seems to depict a poetic reality: it relies essentially on observation of the richness of the natural world. Leaves and flowers enhance the designs with an immediately perceptible sense of movement and fragrance. Geometry, however, is also there to give a structure that is not apparent at first glance, the structural lines being provided by the thin stems and tendrils. The Persian School has contributed an art of great inventiveness and variety.

Die persische Schule bietet uns, im Gegensatz zu der des Maghreb, auf den ersten Blick eine poetische Wirklichkeit. Sie stützt sich im wesentlichen auf die Betrachtung einer äußeren Welt, die von der Natur bereichert wird. In Blättern und Blumen liegen die Bewegung und der »Duft« einer unmittelbar verständlichen Ornamentik. Die Geometrie dient dazu, eine nicht deutlich erkennbare Struktur zu betonen. Diese Struktur entsteht in der Tat aus den zarten Teilen der Verzierung (Stiele und Ranken). Die persische Schule zeigt hierin viel Erfindungsreichtum und ein ausgedehntes Repertoire.

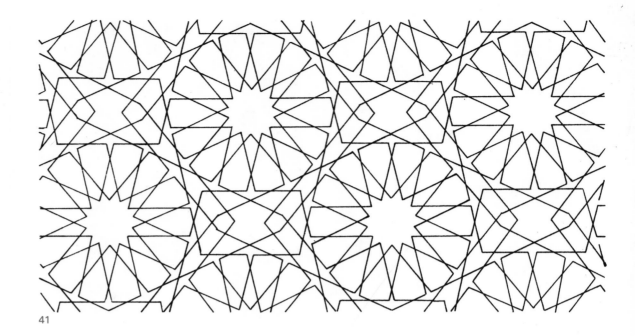

41

41 Epure d'un réseau dont les figures 42, 43, 44 et 45 donnent quatre possibilités de lecture. Par un examen attentif, il est aisé d'en découvrir encore beaucoup d'autres.
42 Lecture de l'étoile extérieure au centre du motif définissant le réseau. Il est à remarquer ici que cette étoile comporte sept branches, ce qui est peu fréquent.
43 Etoiles centrales et extérieures à 14 branches. Pour une même rosace, deux lectures sont donc possible.

41 Diagram of a pattern of which Figs. 42, 43, 44 and 45 give four possible visual interpretations. Close examination reveals many others.
42 The outer star central to the design is shown here. It has seven points, which is very rare.
43 Inner and outer stars with fourteen points. Two visual interpretations of the same rosette are possible.

41 Entwurf eines Geflechts, das in den Figuren 42, 43, 44 und 45 vier Auslegungsmöglichkeiten bietet. Bei aufmerksamer Betrachtung können noch zahlreiche weitere Auslegungen entdeckt werden.
42 Der äußere Stern in der Mitte des geflechtbestimmenden Motivs. Auffallend ist, daß dieser Stern sieben Spitzen hat, was sehr selten vorkommt.
43 Innerer und äußerer Stern mit vierzehn Spitzen. Es sind demnach für dieselbe Rosette zwei Auslegungen möglich.

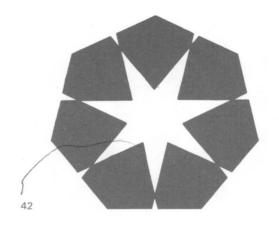

42

43

A chacune de ces deux écoles correspondent des principes de construction et de structure. Quoique, dans l'une et l'autre, les réalisations ornementales puissent paraître extrêmement complexes et indéchiffrables, les bases en sont simples et claires. Le carré, par ses agencements inventifs (Fig. 5-7), définit toutes les figures polygonales, les plus exploitées, aux multiples de 4. Le cercle, par sa division, donne naissance au triangle et aux étoiles. Automatiquement son répertoire sera constitué par les figures définies par les multiples de 3.
Il faut ajouter les figures géométriques

Each of the schools has its own principles of construction and structure. Although the designs produced may appear extremely complex and almost indecipherable, the basic forms are simple and clear.
The square, because of the scope it provides for creative designs (Figs. 5 to 7), is used as the structural unit for all the polygonal figures, most commonly in multiples of four. The circle, because of its divisibility, gives rise to triangles and star shapes. It automatically lends itself to the creation of figures in multiples of three.
Polygonal figures in multiples of five and

Zu jeder dieser beiden Schulen gehören feste Aufbau- und Strukturprinzipien. Obwohl die ornamentalen Ausführungen in beiden äußerst komplex erscheinen können, sind ihre Grundlagen einfach und klar. Das Quadrat bestimmt durch erfinderische Anordnungen alle polygonalen Figuren im Vielfachen von 4; sie kommen am häufigsten vor (Fig. 5 bis 7). Aus dem Kreis entstehen durch seine Teilung Dreiecke und Sterne und eine Vielfalt weiterer Figuren, die durch das Vielfache von 3 gebildet werden.
Zu nennen sind noch die eher seltenen, durch 5 und 7 teilbaren polygonalen

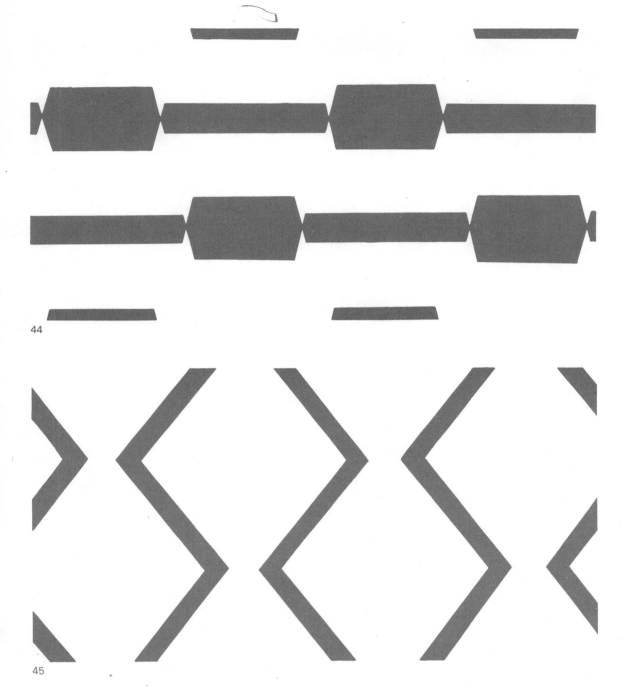

44

45

44 L'épure, en figure 41, livre également la lecture de motifs horizontaux.
45 Les rythmes en zigzag encadrant les rosaces deviennent évidents.

44 *Horizontal motifs also form a part of this design (see Fig. 41).*
45 *Zig-zag lines framing the rosettes.*

44 Der Entwurf in Figur 41 läßt ebenfalls waagrechte Motive erkennen.
45 Hier werden die Zickzack-Rhythmen sichtbar, die die Rosette umrahmen.

polygonales divisibles par 5 et 7 (Fig. 42) qui sont peu fréquentes.
L'ovale et l'ove (Fig. 9 et 10) sont les bases de construction essentielles de la décoration végétale et fleurie. La structure est assurée par la spirale (Fig. 11 et 12) et la sinusoïde (Fig. 13 à 17). Les variantes de leur construction donnent un éventail de possibilités considérable, notamment dans les rinceaux.

seven are also to be found (Fig. 42), but infrequently. The oval and the ovum (Figs. 9 and 10) are used as the structural units for plant and floral decoration. The structural lines here are provided by the spiral (Figs. 11 and 12) and the sinusoid (Figs. 13 to 17). The variants of these constructions give a considerable range of possibilities, particularly in foliage decorations.

geometrischen Figuren (Fig. 42).
Das Oval und die Eiform (Fig. 9 und 10) sind die wesentlichen Grundformen für die pflanzlichen und floralen Ornamente. Die Spirale (Fig. 11 und 12) und die Sinuskurve (Fig. 13 bis 17) geben der Form eine feste Grundlage. Variationen im Aufbau schaffen zahlreiche Möglichkeiten, besonders für die Gestaltung des Laubwerks.

46 Réseau d'entrelacs dont la clef est don-
née en figure 48.
47 Lecture possible par les étoiles à six
branches et leur rythme de répartition.

46 Interlaced tracery. The key is given in Fig.
48.
47 Possible interpretation provided by six-
point stars distributed in a certain pattern.

46 Flechtwerk, dessen Aufschlüsselung
Figur 48 gibt.
47 Die durch sechszackige Sterne und ihre
besondere Anordnung mögliche Auslegung.

46

47

48

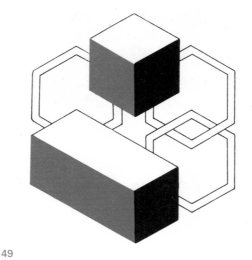

49

L'art ornemental arabe a certes subi les influences romaines, hellénistiques, byzantines et coptes, voire chinoises (en Orient), mais les artistes lui ont donné son identité en recréant, avec beaucoup d'invention, un monde nouveau (Fig. 20 à 25). C'est ainsi que sont nés les agencements d'entrelacs les plus fabuleux et la suggestion d'une troisième dimension créant un espace de lectures multiples. Les subtilités de ces deux éléments n'ont pas échappé à des artistes contemporains, tels que Escher et Vasarely, qui les ont systématiquement exploitées (Fig. 25, 33, 121, 236, 238 et 239).

Les artistes arabes font preuve d'une grande imagination non seulement dans la création des motifs, mais surtout dans leur agencement (Fig. 27 à 29). La lecture d'un motif est la lecture de sa forme. Celle-ci est définie par l'intérieur (Fig. 30) aussi bien que par l'extérieur (Fig. 31). L'ornementation arabe nous astreint, dans la plupart des cas, à lire les deux. Cette méthode d'appréhension nous permet réellement de pénétrer cet art.

La contrepartie, définie par une forme extérieure identique à la forme intérieure d'un motif (Fig. 32 à 35), nous livre une de ces règles du jeu dont nous avons précédemment parlé. Elle ouvre la voie à un infini de possibilités...

Islamic ornamental art does, it is true, bear traces of Roman, Hellenistic, Byzantine and Coptic influence, not to mention Chinese influence (in the east), too, but the Arab artists have given it an identity of its own and created a new world (Figs. 20 to 25). They have developed the most astonishing tracery patterns, which hint at a third dimension, and make possible many different visual interpretations. The subtleties of these two elements have not escaped contemporary artists, like Maurits Corneille Escher and Victor Vasarely, who have used them systematically (Figs. 25, 33, 121, 236, 238 and 239).

Islamic artists show great imagination, not only in the creation of the motifs themselves, but also in the patterns they create from them (Figs. 27 to 29). To analyse a design means looking closely at its form. Islamic ornamentation usually requires an examination of both inner (Fig. 30) and outer (Fig. 31) forms for a really profound appreciation of its qualities.

A reciprocal pattern, produced when the outer form of a motif is the same as the inner (Figs. 32 to 35), illustrates one of the structural rules, and an infinite number of creative possibilities arise from it.

Die arabische Ornamentkunst war römischen, hellenistischen, byzantinischen und koptischen Einflüssen (im Orient) ausgesetzt. Doch die Künstler haben ihr eine eigene Identität gegeben, indem sie mit viel Erfindungsgeist eine neue Welt schufen (Fig. 20 bis 25).
So entstanden hervorragende Beispiele kalligraphischer und geometrischer Flechtwerke mit Andeutung einer dritten Dimension, die Raum für verschiedene Betrachtungsweisen schafft. Die Feinheiten dieser beiden Elemente sind zeitgenössischen Künstlern wie Escher und Vasarely nicht entgangen; diese nutzten sie systematisch aus (Fig. 25, 33, 121, 236, 238 und 239).

Die arabischen Künstler beweisen ihre Erfindungsgabe nicht nur bei der Bildung der Motive, sondern vor allem in deren Anordnung (Fig. 27 bis 29). Das Lesen eines Motivs ist das Lesen seiner Form, die sowohl vom Inneren (Fig. 30) wie vom Äußeren (Fig. 31) bestimmt wird.
In den meisten Fällen sind wir gezwungen, beide Formen zu lesen. Erst diese Methode der Annäherung erlaubt es, wirklich in jene Kunst einzudringen.

Das Spiegelverfahren, bei dem die äußere Form mit der inneren Form des Motivs identisch ist (Fig. 32–35), zeigt eine der Regeln des Spiels, von dem vorher die Rede war, und eröffnet unendliche Möglichkeiten...

50 La feuille de vigne apparaît fréquemment dans les compositions décoratives. Elle est, ici, assez proche de la nature.
51 Par sa stylisation, la feuille de vigne tend à se confondre avec les rinceaux qui la portent.
52 Différents types de formes de feuilles, ou palmes.

50 *The vine leaf is common in decorative art. Here it is represented fairly naturally.*
51 *In stylized form, the vine leaf tends to merge with the stems on which it is borne.*
52 *Different leaf and palm shapes.*

50 Das Weinblatt ist ein häufiges Dekorelement. Hier erscheint es in einer ziemlich naturnahen Gestalt.
51 Durch die Stilisierung scheint es, daß das Weinblatt mit dem Rankenornament, von dem es getragen wird, verschmilzt.
52 Verschiedene Typen von Blattformen oder Palmen.

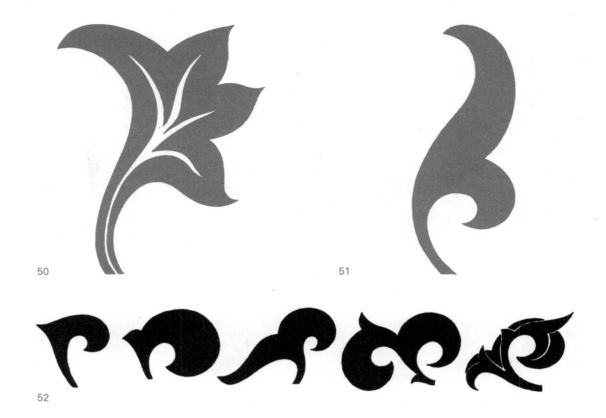

50

51

52

L'agencement du ou des motifs, en fonction d'un tout, forme un réseau (Fig. 36, 40, 41 et 46). Pour «décrypter» un réseau, il suffit d'isoler, en cherchant leur centre, les figures qui le composent (Fig. 37, 42 et 48). La juxtaposition de ces figures crée de nouveaux motifs et de nouveaux rythmes. Il en découle des possibilités de lecture multiples auxquelles la polychromie n'est, de loin, pas étrangère. Nous sommes ainsi dans un monde merveilleux de découvertes.

Au même titre que les figures géométriques constituent le répertoire de la décoration polygonale, un certain nombre d'éléments constitue celui de la décoration végétale et fleurie:
La feuille qui connaît une variété de forme étendue, forme modifiée au gré des dynasties qui en déterminent le style.

The arrangement of the motif or motifs into a whole gives the pattern or tracery (Figs. 36, 40, 41 and 46). 'Deciphering' a pattern is a question of isolating the figures of which it is composed by finding their centres (Figs. 37, 42 and 48). The juxtaposition of the figures creates new motifs and new patterns. There are numerous keys to the interpretation of these patterns, polychromy being a common one. A whole world lies waiting to be discovered.

Just as polygonal design is composed of certain geometric figures, plant and floral design, which is essentially oriental, as we have seen, is composed of certain plants and flowers. Leaves are depicted in different ways, the style being modified according to the taste of each dynasty. Vine leaves (Figs. 50, 51, 61 and 62), palm

Die Anordnung der Motive zu einem Ganzen bildet ein Netz (Fig. 36, 40, 41 und 46). Um dieses Netz zu »entwirren«, genügt es, die Figuren, aus denen es besteht, von der Mitte her zu isolieren (Fig. 37, 42 und 48). Die Nebeneinanderstellung dieser Figuren bildet neue Motive und neue Rhythmen. Daraus ergeben sich zahllose Möglichkeiten der Auslegung und Entdeckungen, vielgestaltig und bunt wie die Welt der Polychromie.

So, wie die geometrischen Figuren das »Repertoire« der polygonalen Dekoration bilden, sind bestimmte Elemente die Grundlage der für den Orient typischen pflanzlichen und floralen Dekoration. Das Blatt hat viele Ausdrucksformen, die sich im Laufe der Dynastien, welche seinen jeweiligen Stil bestimmen, wandeln: Weinblätter (Fig. 50, 51, 61 und 62),

53

54

53, 54   Les palmettes s'ajoutent au répertoire étendu des végétaux.
55, 56   Les coquilles ou rosaces sont parfois très proches et issues des palmettes.

53, 54   *Palmettes (palm-shaped designs) form part of the extensive repertoire of plant motifs.*
55, 56   *Shells and rosettes often resemble palmettes and are created from them.*

53–54   Palmetten gehören zum ausgedehnten »Repertoire« an Pflanzen.
55–56   Muscheln und Rosetten gehen aus den Palmetten hervor und sind sich manchmal sehr ähnlich.

55

56

Feuilles de vigne (Fig. 50, 51, 61 et 62), palmes (Fig. 52), palmettes (Fig. 53 et 54), rosaces et coquilles, issues des palmettes, (Fig. 55 et 56), feuilles d'acanthe (Fig. 56 et 60). Ce répertoire se complète par les fleurons (Fig. 57 et 58) et la fameuse pomme de pin (Fig. 63).
Les fleurs, variées dans leur espèce (entre autres l'œillet, la pivoine, la tulipe et la rose) le sont également dans leur interprétation (Fig. 64 à 71).

leaves (Fig. 52) and palm-shaped designs or palmettes (Figs. 53 and 54), rosettes and shells (Figs. 55 and 56), which are derived from palmettes, and acanthus leaves (Figs. 56 and 60) are all used. Fleurons (Figs. 57 and 58) and the famous pine-cone (Fig. 63) complete the repertoire. A variety of flowers (especially carnations, peonies, tulips and roses) are also depicted and are treated in different ways (Figs. 64 to 71).

Palmen (Fig. 52), Palmetten (Fig. 53 und 54), Rosetten und Muscheln, entwickelt aus den Palmetten (Fig. 55 und 56), und Akanthusblätter (Fig. 56 und 60). Dieses »Repertoire« wird ergänzt durch Blütenblätter (Fig. 57 und 58) und durch den berühmten Tannenzapfen (Fig. 63).
Die Blumen, unter anderen die Nelke, die Pfingstrose, die Tulpe und die Rose, variieren nach ihrer Gattung und nach der Art der Darstellung (Fig. 64 bis 71).

57, 58 La palme simple à laquelle s'ajoute, à la base, un culot de plus en plus important, devient fleuron.

59, 60 L'acanthe dont l'origine romaine est évidente à Cordoue (Fig. 60) devient par sa stylisation plus byzantine (Fig. 59).

61, 62 Evolution de la feuille de vigne proche de la nature (Fig. 61, Kairouan IXe siècle) qui, sous l'influence almohade, devient palme (Fig. 62).

57, 58 Simple palm with a base that becomes larger and turns into a fleuron.

59, 60 The acanthus of Roman origin seen at Cordoba (Fig. 60) becomes more Byzantine when stylized (Fig. 59).

61, 62 The vine leaf, naturally depicted (Fig. 61, Qairawan, 9th century), becomes a palm under Almohad influence (Fig. 62).

57–58 Die einfache Palme wird zum Blütenblatt, indem ihre untere, stengelartige Verzierung immer mehr wächst.

59–60 Das Akanthusblatt, dessen römischer Ursprung in Cordoba deutlich ist (Fig. 60), erhält durch Stilisierung eher byzantinische Züge (Fig. 59).

61–62 Entwicklung des naturnahen Weinblattes (Fig. 61, Kairuan, 9. Jh.), das unter almohadischem Einfluß zur Palme wird (Fig. 62).

57

58

59

60

61

62

63

63 La pomme de pin que représente cette figure est assez caractéristique. Elle peut, suivant les lieux, prendre des formes plus allongées, voire ondulantes.

63 A fairly characteristic representation of a pine-cone. Depending on its place of origin, it may become more elongated or flowing in form.

63 Der hier abgebildete Tannenzapfen ist charakteristisch. Er kann, je nach Ort, eine länglichere oder sogar wellige Gestalt annehmen.

La décoration des surfaces par ces divers motifs est structurée généralement par les éléments grêles des motifs répartis de façon symétrique ou asymétrique (Fig. 72 et 73). La décoration végétale et fleurie se distingue par un riche foisonnement d'éléments décoratifs répartis souvent avec une très grande fantaisie. C'est le domaine, par excellence, de la frise et de l'encadrement.

Il nous est apparu indispensable de compléter ces deux types de décoration par une manifestation de l'art arabe peu connue et peu exploitée, l'apparition fugitive de l'élément humain et animal. Cette figuration est pourtant réprouvée et interdite par le Prophète, «celui qui a fait une image sera mis en demeure, au jour de la Résurrection, de lui insuffler une âme, mais il ne pourra pas le faire...» stipulent les hadits.
La figuration d'êtres vivants n'est pas fréquente, en effet, elle existe néanmoins, principalement en Orient, en Egypte et en Italie du Sud.

The structure for these different motifs is generally provided by the symmetrical or asymmetrical arrangement of fine lines (Figs. 72 and 73). Floral and plant decorations are enhanced by a rich mass of decorative lines, often arranged with great imagination. These designs belong pre-eminently to frieze and frame ornamentation.

In addition to the two types of ornamental design described above, it is essential to mention an element in Islamic art which is little known and very rare: the fleeting appearance of human beings and animals, the portrayal of which was censured and forbidden by the Prophet Muhammad. 'He who creates an image will be called upon, on the Day of the Judgement, to breathe into it a soul, but he will not be able to....' (according to the Hadith or Traditions). Living creatures are indeed rarely depicted. When they are depicted, it is mainly in the east, in Egypt and in southern Italy.

Die Ausschmückung der Flächen wird meist von den symmetrisch oder asymmetrisch verteilten, sehr feinen Motivteilen bestimmt (Fig. 72 und 73). Die pflanzliche und florale Dekoration zeichnet sich durch eine Überfülle an Schmuckelementen aus, die oft mit viel Phantasie angeordnet sind; sie kommen vor allem an Friesen und in Umrahmungen zur Anwendung.

Es schien unerläßlich, diese beiden Typen der Dekoration zu ergänzen durch eine wenig bekannte und kaum angewandte Ausdrucksform der arabischen Kunst: das flüchtige Auftreten des menschlichen und tierischen Elements. Solche Darstellungen wurden nämlich vom Propheten mißbilligt und verboten: »Am Tage des Gerichts wird derjenige, der ein Bildnis hergestellt hat, aufgefordert werden, diesem den Lebensatem einzuhauchen, aber er wird es nicht vermögen...« sagen ausdrücklich die Hadith-Überlieferungen.
Die Darstellung von Lebewesen ist tatsächlich nicht häufig, aber sie kommt dennoch vor, besonders im Orient, in Ägypten und in Süditalien.

64, 65, 66 Dans la décoration fleurie, l'œillet occupe une place importante, sous des aspects très variés.
67, 68 La tulipe donne lieu à une stylisation intéressante et très poussée.

64, 65, 66 The carnation occupies an important place in floral decoration, and it is given many different forms.
67, 68 Tulips are used as the basis for an interesting and extremely elaborate stylization.

64–65–66 Im floralen Dekor kommt der Nelke in verschiedenen Erscheinungsformen eine wichtige Rolle zu.
67–68 Die Tulpe ermöglicht eine interessante und hochentwickelte Stilisierung.

64

65

66

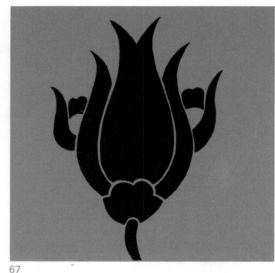

67

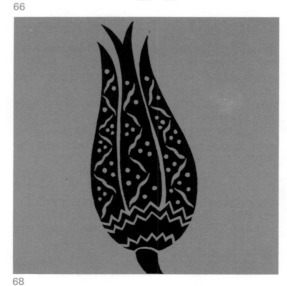

68

69

69, 70, 71 La rose donne lieu, dans son interprétation graphique, à une grande fantaisie.

72, 73 Il est à noter que la structure des compositions végétales et florales peut être de base symétrique (Fig. 72) ou asymétrique (Fig. 73).

69, 70, 71 Roses are depicted with great imagination.
72, 73 The structural lines of plant and floral designs may be either symmetrical (Fig. 72) or asymmetrical (Fig. 73).

69—70—71 Die Rose zeigt in ihrer graphischen Ausführung viel Phantasie.
72—73 Die Struktur der pflanzlichen und floralen Kompositionen kann eine symmetrische (Fig. 72) oder asymmetrische (Fig. 73) Grundlage haben.

70

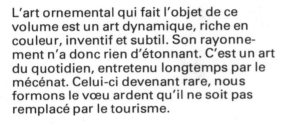

71

L'art ornemental qui fait l'objet de ce volume est un art dynamique, riche en couleur, inventif et subtil. Son rayonnement n'a donc rien d'étonnant. C'est un art du quotidien, entretenu longtemps par le mécénat. Celui-ci devenant rare, nous formons le vœu ardent qu'il ne soit pas remplacé par le tourisme.

Islamic ornamental art is dynamic, richly colourful, inventive and subtle. Its attractiveness for many people comes therefore as no surprise. It is an art that belongs to everyday existence, an art long supported by patronage. It is devoutly hoped that, patronage having almost died out, it will not be replaced by tourism.

Die Ornamentik, welche das vorliegende Buch zum Thema hat, ist eine dynamische Kunst, farbenfreudig, erfindungsreich und verfeinert. Ihre weite Verbreitung hat somit nichts Erstaunliches an sich. Es ist eine Kunst des Alltags, die lange Zeit vom Mäzenatentum getragen und erhalten wurde. Da dieser alte Brauch immer seltener wird, ist nur zu hoffen, daß an seiner Stelle nicht der moderne Tourismus zum alleinigen Träger und materiellen Förderer wird.

72

73

Ecriture, calligraphie et épigraphie

Maîtrise et assurance
L'invention est présente
parce que tout est permis.

Script, Calligraphy and Epigraphy

Mastery and self-assurance.
Inventiveness is born of
total freedom.

Kalligraphie und Inschriften

Meisterschaft und Sicherheit.
Weil alles erlaubt ist,
ist Erfindungsgabe vorhanden.

74 Composition calligraphique, écriture double, XIXe siècle.

74 *Calligraphy with double letters, 19th century.*

74 Kalligraphischer Schriftdekor, Doppelschrift, 19. Jh.

75 Composition calligraphique.
76 Maroc, Fès, médersa Bou Inaniya, composition épigraphique, plâtre sculpté, XIVᵉ siècle.
77 Turquie, Istanbul, mosquée des Princes, composition épigraphique, carreaux de faïence.
78 Turquie, Istanbul, mosquée des Princes, composition épigraphique, carreaux de faïence.

75 *Calligraphy.*
76 *Morocco: Fez, Madrasah of Bu Inaniyya. Epigraphy, stucco, 14th century.*
77 *Turkey: Istanbul, Mosque of the Princes. Epigraphy, tin-glazed earthenware tiles.*
78 *Turkey: Istanbul, Mosque of the Princes. Epigraphy, tin-glazed earthenware tiles.*

75 Kalligraphischer Schriftdekor.
76 Marokko, Fez, Medrese Bu Inaniya, Inschriftendekor, Stuck, geschnitten, 14. Jh.
77 Türkei, Istanbul, Prinzenmoschee, Inschriftendekor, Fliesen, Fayence.
78 Türkei, Istanbul, Prinzenmoschee, Inschriftendekor, Fliesen, Fayence.

75

76

77

78

79

80

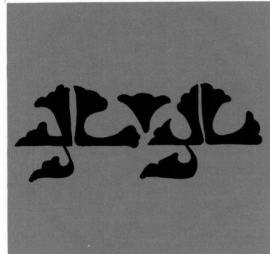

81

82

83

84

85 Composition calligraphique koufique, nom propre de Mahmoud Yazir autour de la lettre «m».
86 Composition calligraphique à partir des noms d'Ali et de Mahomet.
87 Turquie, bois sculpté, composition en lettre koufique.
88 Composition calligraphique koufique.
89 Composition calligraphique koufique, le nom de Mahomet est répété quatre fois.
90 Composition calligraphique koufique «Dieu soit loué».

85 Kufic calligraphic design: the name Mahmud Yazir constructed around the letter 'm'.
86 Calligraphic design based on the names of Ali and Muhammad.
87 Turkey. Carved wood, design composed of Kufic characters.
88 Kufic calligraphy.
89 Kufic calligraphic design, in which the name Muhammad appears four times.
90 Kufic calligraphy: 'Praise be to God.'

85 Kufischer Schriftdekor, der Name Mahmud Yasir, um den Buchstaben »m« angeordnet.
86 Kalligraphischer Schriftdekor, ausgehend von den Namen Ali und Mohammed.
87 Türkei, Holz, geschnitzt, Dekor in Kufi-Schriftzeichen.
88 Kufischer Schriftdekor.
89 Kufischer Schriftdekor, der Name Mohammeds ist viermal wiederholt.
90 Kufischer Schriftdekor, »Gott sei gelobt«.

85

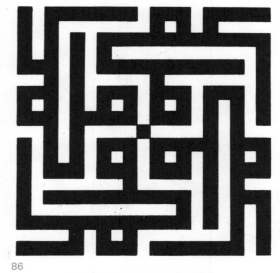

86

87

88

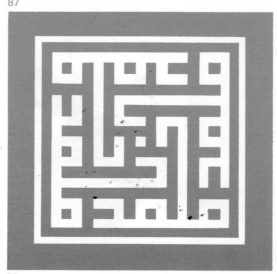

89

90

91 Lettre monogramme, style sumbuli.
92 Lettre monogramme, style sumbuli.
93 Lettre monogramme, style sumbuli.
94 Lettre monogramme, style sumbuli.
95 Lettre monogramme, style sumbuli.
96 Lettre monogramme, style sumbuli.

91 *Monogram initial, Sumbuli style.*
92 *Monogram initial, Sumbuli style.*
93 *Monogram initial, Sumbuli style.*
94 *Monogram initial, Sumbuli style.*
95 *Monogram initial, Sumbuli style.*
96 *Monogram initial, Sumbuli style.*

91 Monogramm-Buchstabe, Sumbulistil.
92 Monogramm-Buchstabe, Sumbulistil.
93 Monogramm-Buchstabe, Sumbulistil.
94 Monogramm-Buchstabe, Sumbulistil.
95 Monogramm-Buchstabe, Sumbulistil.
96 Monogramm-Buchstabe, Sumbulistil.

91

92

93

94

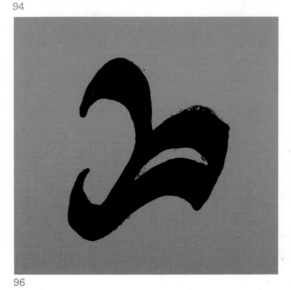

95

96

98

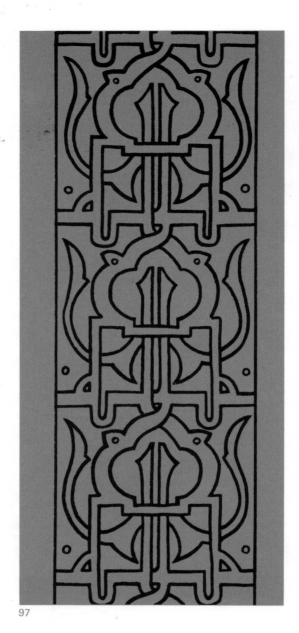

97

99

100

101

102 Composition calligraphique koufique.

102 Kufic calligraphy.

102 Kufischer Schriftdekor.

103 Afghanistan, composition calligraphique en koufi tressé, Coran du XVIIIe siècle.
104 Composition calligraphique koufique.

103 Afghanistan. Calligraphic design in twined Kufic characters, 18th-century Koran.
104 Kufic calligraphy.

103 Afghanistan, kalligraphischer Schriftdekor in geflochtenem Kufi, Koran des 18. Jh.
104 Kufischer Schriftdekor.

103

104

105

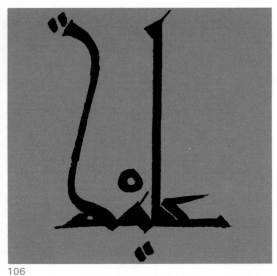

106

107

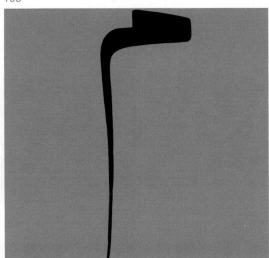

108

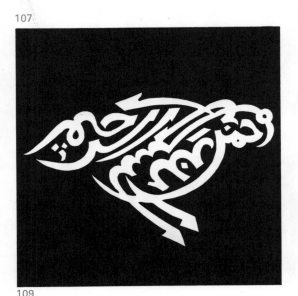

109

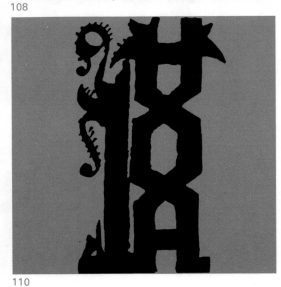

110

105 Composition calligraphique en forme de visage humain.
106 Calligraphie.
107 Lettre «f» en écriture koufique.
108 Lettre finale «M».
109 Composition calligraphique en forme d'oiseau.
110 Composition calligraphique, le nom d'Allah en koufi tressé.

105 *Calligraphic design in the shape of a human face.*
106 *Calligraphy.*
107 *Letter 'f' in Kufic script.*
108 *Final 'm'.*
109 *Calligraphic design in the shape of a bird.*
110 *Calligraphic design: the name Allah in entwined Kufic characters.*

105 Kalligraphischer Schriftdekor in Gestalt eines menschlichen Gesichts.
106 Kalligraphie.
107 Buchstabe »f« in kufischer Schrift.
108 Endbuchstabe »M«.
109 Kalligraphischer Schriftdekor in Gestalt eines Vogels.
110 Kalligraphischer Schriftdekor, der Name Allahs in geflochtenem Kufi.

111

112

113

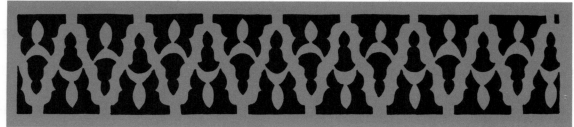

114

115

Motifs ornementaux géométriques sans entrelacs
Surprenants de rigueur et d'originalité, sous des dehors apparemment simples.

Geometric Ornamental Motifs
Astonishing precision and originality behind apparent simplicity

Geometrische Ornament-Motive ohne Flechtwerk
Überraschende Genauigkeit und Originalität unter scheinbar einfachem Äußeren.

116   Maroc, Fès, mosaïque de faïence, XXᵉ siècle.

116   Morocco: Fez. Tin-glazed earthenware mosaic, 20th century.

116   Marokko, Fez, Fayencemosaik, 20. Jh.

117 Syrie, Damas, musée national, salle damascène, bois sculpté et peint, XVIIIᵉ siècle.
118 Syrie, Damas, mosquée des Omeyyades, marbre incrusté.
119 Maroc mosaïque de faïence.
120 Espagne, Séville, Alcazar, mosaïque de faïence, XIVᵉ siècle.

117 Syria: National Museum, Damascus, Damascan Room. Carved and painted wood, 18th century.
118 Syria: Umayyad Mosque. Inlaid marble.
119 Morocco. Tin-glazed earthenware mosaic.
120 Spain: Seville, Alcazar. Tin-glazed earthenware mosaic, 14th century.

117 Syrien, Damaskus, Nationalmuseum, Damaszenersaal, Holz, geschnitzt und bemalt, 18. Jh.
118 Syrien, Omaijadenmoschee, Marmor, eingelegt.
119 Marokko, Fayencemosaik.
120 Spanien, Sevilla, Alcazar, Fayencemosaik, 14. Jh.

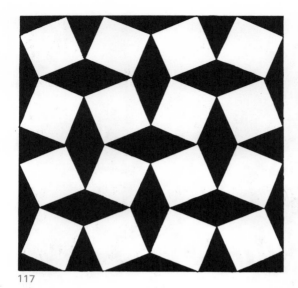

117

118

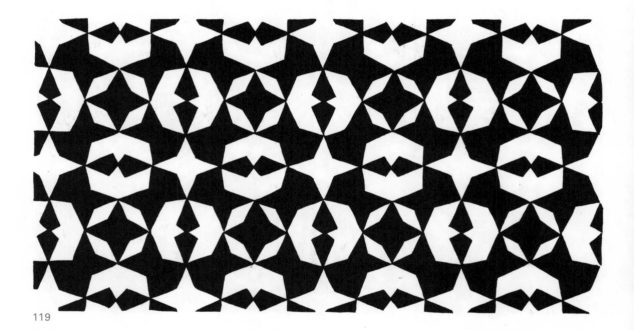

119

120

121

122

123

124

125

121 Tunisie, Tunis, Dar Lajimi, mosaïque de faïence, XVIIe siècle.
122 Syrie, Damas, mosquée des Omeyyades, marbre incrusté.
123 Maroc, Tétouan, jardin public, mosaïque de faïence, XXe siècle.
124 Egypte, Le Caire, palais de Radwan Bey, mosaïque de marbre, XVIIe siècle.
125 Syrie, Damas, mosquée des Omeyyades, marbre incrusté.

121 Tunisia: Tunis, Dar Lajimi. Tin-glazed earthenware mosaic, 17th century.
122 Syria: Damascus, Umayyad Mosque. Inlaid marble.
123 Morocco: Tetuan, public gardens. Tinglazed earthenware mosaic, 20th century.
124 Egypt: Cairo, Palace of Radwan Bey. Marble mosaic, 17th century.
125 Syria: Damascus, Umayyad Mosque. Inlaid marble.

121 Tunesien, Tunis, Dar Lajimi, Fayencemosaik, 17. Jh.
122 Syrien, Damaskus, Omaijadenmoschee, Marmor, eingelegt.
123 Marokko, Tetuan, öffentlicher Garten, Fayencemosaik, 20. Jh.
124 Ägypten, Kairo, Palast des Radwan Bey, Marmormosaik, 17. Jh.
125 Syrien, Damaskus, Omaijadenmoschee, Marmor, eingelegt.

126 Egypte, bibliothèque du Caire, enluminure de Coran.
127 Syrie, Damas, marbre incrusté, XXᵉ
siècle.
128 Syrie, Damas, mosquée al-Aqsab,
marbre incrusté, XIVᵉ siècle.
129 Egypte, Le Caire, musée arabe, bois
sculpté, Xᵉ siècle.
130 Perse, céramique, VIIᵉ siècle.
131 Egypte, Le Caire, musée arabe, bois
sculpté, IXᵉ-Xᵉ siècle.

*126 Egypt: National Library, Cairo. Koran
illumination.*
*127 Syria: Damascus. Inlaid marble, 20th
century.*
*128 Syria: Damascus, Mosque of al-Aqsab.
Inlaid marble, 14th century.*
*129 Egypt: Museum of Islamic Art, Cairo.
Carved wood, 10th century.*
130 Iran. Ceramic design, 7th century.
*131 Egypt: Museum of Islamic Art, Cairo.
Carved wood, 9th–10th century.*

126 Ägypten, Bibliothek von Kairo, Miniatur
zum Koran.
127 Syrien, Damaskus, Marmor, eingelegt,
20. Jh.
128 Syrien, Damaskus, Moschee al-Aqsab,
Marmor, eingelegt, 14. Jh.
129 Ägypten, Kairo, Islamisches Museum,
Holz, geschnitzt, 10. Jh.
130 Persien, Keramik, 7. Jh.
131 Ägypten, Kairo, Islamisches Museum,
Holz, geschnitzt, 9.–10. Jh.

126

127

128

129

130

131

132

132 Perse, céramique, XIIIᵉ siècle.
133 Iran, Ispahan, médersa du sultan Hussein, mosaïque de faïence, XVIIᵉ siècle.
134 Egypte, Le Caire, médersa du sultan Baybars, pierre sculptée, XIIIᵉ siècle.

132 *Iran. Ceramic design, 13th century.*
133 *Iran: Isfahan, Madrasah of Shah Sultan Husain. Tin-glazed earthenware mosaic, 17th century.*
134 *Egypt: Cairo, Madrasah of Sultan Beybars. Carved stone, 13th century.*

132 Persien, Keramik, 13. Jh.
133 Iran, Isfahan, Medrese des Sultans Hussein, Fayencemosaik, 17. Jh.
134 Ägypten, Kairo, Medrese des Sultans Baibars, Stein, behauen, 13. Jh.

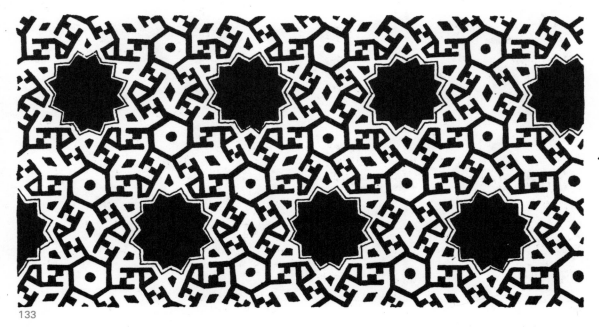

133

134

135 Maroc, mosaïque de faïence.
136 Maroc, mosaïque de faïence.
137 Syrie, musée de Damas, salle damascène, bois peint, XVIIIe siècle.

135 *Morocco. Tin-glazed earthenware mo-*
saic.
136 *Morocco. Tin-glazed earthenware mo-*
saic.
137 *Syria: National Museum, Damascus,*
Damascan Room. Painted wood, 18th
century.

135 Marokko, Fayencemosaik.
136 Marokko, Fayencemosaik.
137 Syrien, Damaskus, Nationalmuseum,
Damaszenersaal, Holz, bemalt, 13. Jh.

135

136

137

138

139

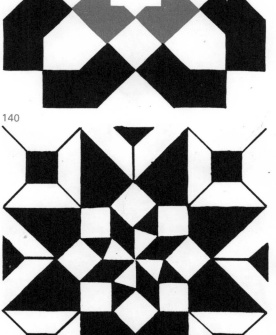

140

141

142

143

138 Maroc, Fès, sanctuaire d'Idris II, mosaïque de faïence.
139 Tunisie, musée du Bardo, mosaïque de faïence.
140 Maroc, Fès, sanctuaire d'Idris II, mosaïque de faïence.
141 Maroc, Fès, mosaïque de faïence, XXᵉ siècle.
142 Egypte, Le Caire, marbre incrusté.
143 Egypte, Le Caire, mosquée el-Aini, marbre incrusté, XVᵉ siècle.

138 *Morocco: Fez, Sanctuary of Idriss II. Tin-glazed earthenware mosaic.*
139 *Tunisia: Bardo Museum, Tunis. Tin-glazed earthenware mosaic.*
140 *Morocco: Fez, Sanctuary of Idriss II. Tin-glazed earthenware mosaic.*
141 *Morocco: Fez. Tin-glazed earthenware mosaic, 20th century.*
142 *Egypt: Cairo. Inlaid marble.*
143 *Egypt: Cairo, Mosque of al-Aini. Inlaid marble, 15th century.*

138 Marokko, Fez, Mausoleum des Idris II., Fayencemosaik.
139 Tunesien, Nationalmuseum im Bardo, Fayencemosaik.
140 Marokko, Fez, Mausoleum des Idris II., Fayencemosaik.
141 Marokko, Fez, Fayencemosaik, 20. Jh.
142 Ägypten, Kairo, Marmor, eingelegt.
143 Ägypten, Kairo, Moschee al-Aini, Marmor, eingelegt, 15. Jh.

144 Tunisie, Tunis, musée du Bardo, mosaïque de faïence.
145 Maroc, mosaïque de faïence.
146 Maroc, Fès, sanctuaire d'Idris II, mosaïque de faïence.
147 Maroc, Fès, sanctuaire d'Idris II, mosaïque de faïence.
148 Maroc, mosaïque de faïence.
149 Maroc, Fès el-Bali, fontaine, mosaïque de faïence.

144 *Tunisia: Bardo Museum, Tunis. Tin-glazed earthenware mosaic.*
145 *Morocco. Tin-glazed earthenware mosaic.*
146 *Morocco: Fez, Sanctuary of Idriss II. Tin-glazed earthenware mosaic.*
147 *Morocco: Fez, Sanctuary of Idriss II. Tin-glazed earthenware mosaic.*
148 *Morocco. Tin-glazed earthenware mosaic.*
149 *Morocco: Fes al-Bali. Fountain, tin-glazed earthenware mosaic.*

144 Tunesien, Nationalmuseum im Bardo, Fayencemosaik.
145 Marokko, Fayencemosaik.
146 Marokko, Fez, Mausoleum des Idris II., Fayencemosaik.
147 Marokko, Fez, Mausoleum des Idris II., Fayencemosaik.
148 Marokko, Fayencemosaik.
149 Marokko, Fez al-Bali, Brunnen, Fayencemosaik.

144

145

146

147

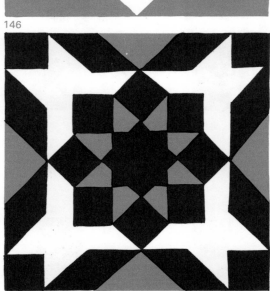

148

149

150

151

152

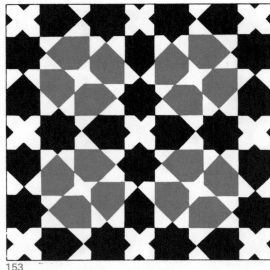

153

154

155

156

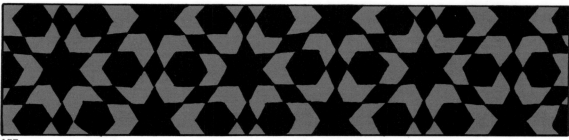

157

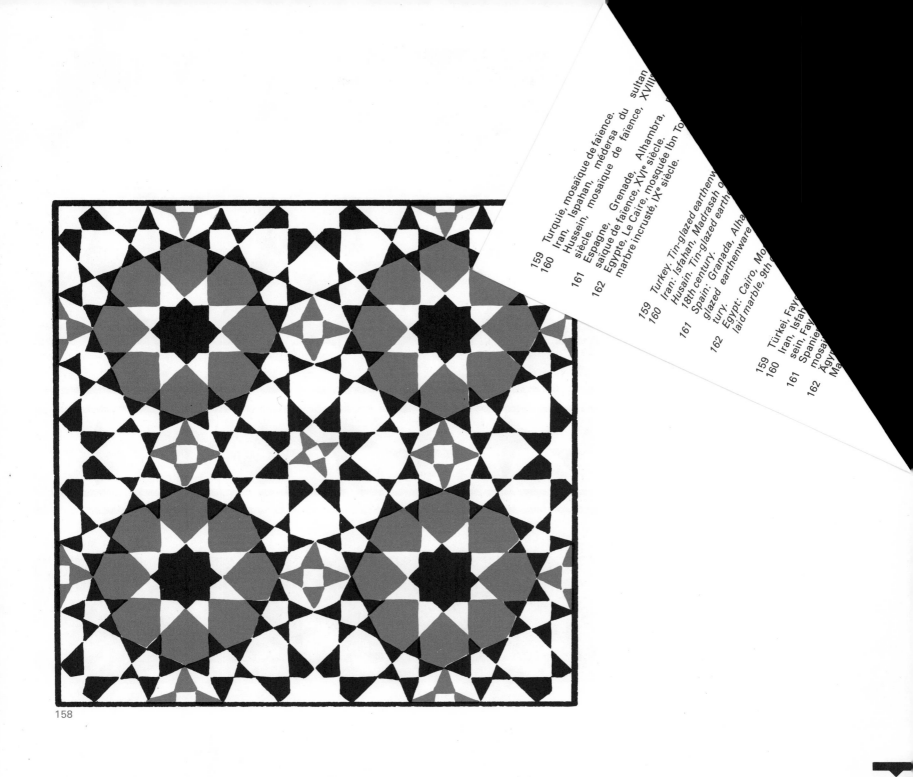

158

...mo-

...uloun,

...are mosaic.
...f Shah Sultan
...enware mosaic,

...mbra Palace. Tin-
...mosaic, 16th cen-

...sque of Ibn Tulun. In-
...century.

...encemosaik.
...an, Medrese des Sultan Hus-
...encemosaik, 18. Jh.
...n, Granada, Alhambra, Fayence-
...k, 16. Jh.
...ten, Kairo, Moschee des Ibn Tulun,
...rmor, eingelegt, 9. Jh.

159

160

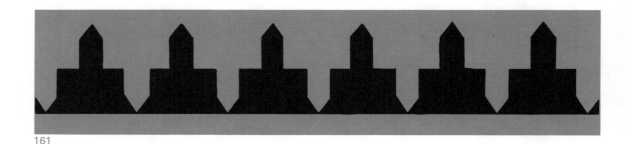

161

162

163

164

165

166

163 Egypte, Le Caire, marbre incrusté, XVᵉ siècle.
164 Syrie, Damas, maison Mardam, marbre incrusté.
165 Syrie, Damas, musée national, salle damascène, marbre incrusté, XVIIIᵉ siècle.
166 Egypte, Le Caire, musée arabe, bois sculpté.

163 *Egypt: Cairo. Inlaid marble, 15th century.*
164 *Syria: Damascus, Mardam House. Inlaid marble.*
165 *Syria: National Museum, Damascus, Damascan Room. Inlaid marble, 18th century.*
166 *Egypt: Museum of Islamic Art, Cairo. Carved wood.*

163 Ägypten, Kairo, Marmor, eingelegt, 15. Jh.
164 Syrien, Damaskus, Haus Mardam, Marmor, eingelegt.
165 Syrien, Damaskus, Nationalmuseum, Damaszenersaal, Marmor, eingelegt, 18. Jh.
166 Ägypten, Kairo, Islamisches Museum, Holz, geschnitzt.

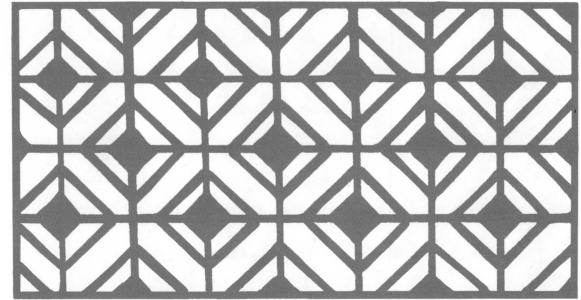

167

168

169

170

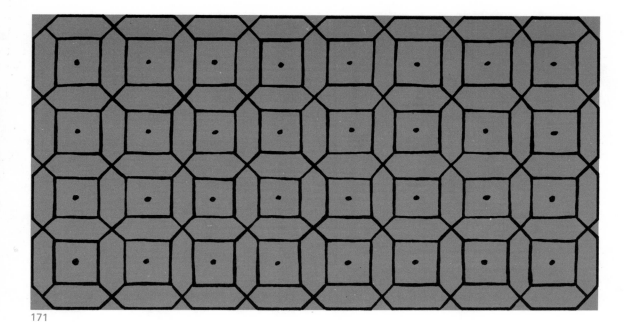

171

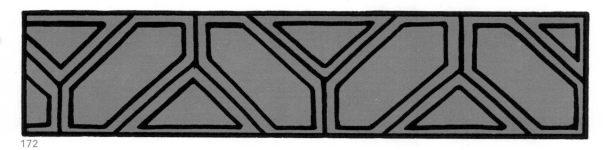

172

173

174

175 Syrie, Damas, mosquée des Omeyyades, marbre incrusté.
176 Maroc, Ouarzazate, plâtre sculpté et peint, XIXᵉ siècle.
177 Egypte, marbre incrusté, XVᵉ siècle.
178 Syrie, Damas, musée national, salle damascène, marbre incrusté, XVIIIᵉ siècle.
179 Inde, ivoire incrusté.

175 *Syria: Damascus, Umayyad Mosque. Inlaid marble.*
176 *Morocco: Ouarzazate. Painted stucco, 19th century.*
177 *Egypt. Inlaid marble, 15th century.*
178 *Syria: National Museum, Damascus, Damascan Room. Inlaid marble, 18th century.*
179 *India. Inlaid ivory.*

175 Syrien, Damaskus, Omaijadenmoschee, Marmor, eingelegt.
176 Marokko, Warzazate, Stuck, geschnitten und bemalt, 19. Jh.
177 Ägypten, Marmor, eingelegt, 15. Jh.
178 Syrien, Damaskus, Nationalmuseum, Damaszenersaal, Marmor, eingelegt, 18. Jh.
179 Indien, Elfenbein, eingelegt.

175

176

177

178

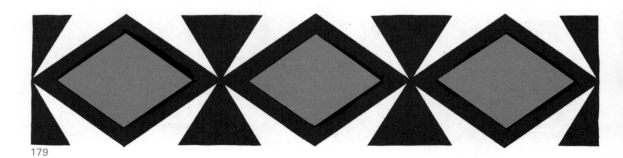
179

180

181

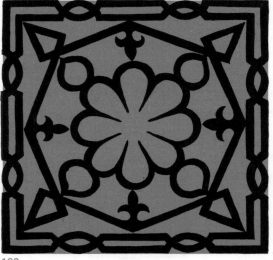

182

183

180 Syrie, Damas, marbre incrusté, XXᵉ siècle.
181 Syrie, Damas, marbre incrusté, XXᵉ siècle.
182 Syrie, Damas, mosquée Sinan Pacha, marbre incrusté, XVIᵉ siècle.
183 Algérie, Tlemcen, mosquée Sidi Bou Médine, plâtre sculpté, XIVᵉ siècle.
184 Syrie, Damas, marbre incrusté, XXᵉ siècle.

180 *Syria: Damascus. Inlaid marble, 20th century.*
181 *Syria: Damascus. Inlaid marble, 20th century.*
182 *Syria: Damascus, Mosque of Sinan Pasha. Inlaid marble, 16th century.*
183 *Algeria: Tlemcen, Mosque of Sidi Bu Medina. Stucco, 14th century.*
184 *Syria: Damascus. Inlaid marble, 20th century.*

180 Syrien, Damaskus, Marmor, eingelegt, 20. Jh.
181 Syrien, Damaskus, Marmor, eingelegt, 20. Jh.
182 Syrien, Damaskus, Moschee des Sinan Pascha, Marmor, eingelegt, 16. Jh.
183 Algerien, Tlemcen, Moschee von Bu Medine, Stuck, geschnitten, 14. Jh.
184 Syrien, Damaskus, Marmor, eingelegt, 20. Jh.

184

185 Maroc, étoffe, XIXe siècle.
186 Syrie, Damas, mosquée des Omeyyades, marbre incrusté.
187 Espagne, Séville, Alcazar, mosaïque de
faïence, XIVe siècle.

185 Morocco. Fabric, 19th century.
186 Syria: Damascus, Umayyad Mosque.
Inlaid marble.
187 Spain: Seville, Alcazar. Tin-glazed
earthenware mosaic, 14th century.

185 Marokko, Stoff, 19. Jh.
186 Syrien, Damaskus, Omaijadenmoschee,
Marmor, eingelegt.
187 Spanien, Sevilla, Alcazar, Fayencemosaik, 14. Jh.

185

186

187

188

189

190

191

192

193

188 Inde, Amber, ivoire et ébène incrustés, XVIIᵉ siècle.
189 Egypte, Le Caire, musée arabe, bois sculpté, XIᵉ siècle.
190 Syrie, Damas, mosquée des Omeyyades, marbre incrusté.
191 Maroc, Chéchaouen, broderie.
192 Maroc, Fès, céramique.
193 Maroc, Fès, étoffe, XIXᵉ siècle.

188 India: Palace of Amber. Inlaid ivory and ebony, 17th century.
189 Egypt: Museum of Islamic Art, Cairo. Carved wood, 11th century.
190 Syria: Damascus, Umayyad Mosque. Inlaid marble.
191 Morocco: Chechaouene. Embroidery.
192 Morocco: Fez. Ceramic design.
193 Morocco: Fez. Fabric, 19th century.

188 Indien, Amber, Elfenbein und Ebenholz, eingelegt, 17. Jh.
189 Ägypten, Kairo, Islamisches Museum, Holz, geschnitzt, 11. Jh.
190 Syrien, Damaskus, Omaijadenmoschee, Marmor, eingelegt.
191 Marokko, Chechuan, Stickerei.
192 Marokko, Fez, Keramik.
193 Marokko, Fez, Stoff, 19. Jh.

194 Egypte, Le Caire, palais de Radwan Bey, marbre incrusté, XVIIᵉ siècle.
195 Turquie, Balikésir, mosquée de Zaganos Pacha, bois sculpté, XVᵉ siècle.
196 Maroc, Tétouan, bois peint, XVIIIᵉ siècle.
197 Espagne, médina az-Zahara, plâtre sculpté, IXᵉ siècle.
198 Syrie, Damas, musée national, salle damascène, marbre incrusté, XVIIIᵉ siècle.

194 *Egypt: Cairo, Palace of Radwan Bey. Inlaid marble, 17th century.*
195 *Turkey: Balıkesir, Mosque of Zaganos Pasha. Carved wood, 15th century.*
196 *Morocco: Tetuan. Painted wood, 18th century.*
197 *Spain: Medina al-Zahara. Stucco, 9th century.*
198 *Syria: National Museum, Damascus, Damascan Room. Inlaid marble, 18th century.*

194 Ägypten, Kairo, Palast des Radwan Bey, Marmor, eingelegt, 17. Jh.
195 Türkei, Balıkesir, Moschee des Zaganos Pascha, Holz, geschnitzt, 15. Jh.
196 Marokko, Tetuan, Holz, bemalt, 18. Jh.
197 Spanien, Medina az-Zahara, Stuck, geschnitten, 9. Jh.
198 Syrien, Damaskus, Nationalmuseum, Damaszenersaal, Marmor, eingelegt, 18. Jh.

194

195

196

197

198

199 Syrie, Damas, musée national, salle damascène, bois sculpté et peint, XVIIIe siècle.

199 Syria: National Museum, Damascus, Damascan Room. Carved and painted wood, 18th century.

199 Syrien, Damaskus, Nationalmuseum, Damaszenersaal, Holz, geschnitzt und bemalt, 18. Jh.

199

200

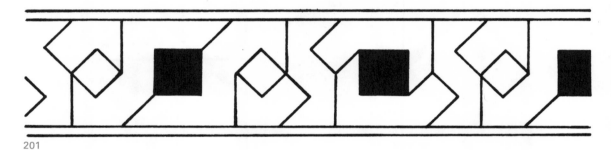

201

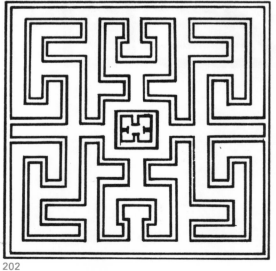

202

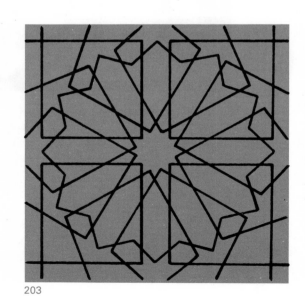

203

204

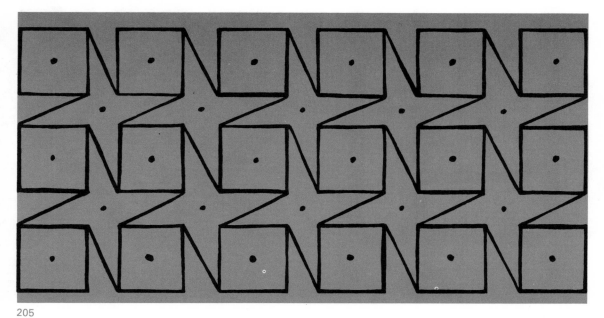

205

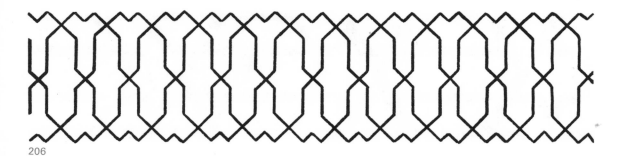

206

207 Tunisie, Tunis, Dar Othman, marbre
    incrusté, XVIIᵉ siècle.
208 Inde, Agra, Tadj Mahall, marbre incrus-
    té, XVIIᵉ siècle.
209 Egypte, Le Caire, musée arabe, bois
    sculpté, XIIᵉ siècle.

207 *Tunisia: Tunis, Dar Othman. Inlaid
    marble, 17th century.*
208 *India: Agra, Taj Mahal. Inlaid marble,
    17th century.*
209 *Egypt: Museum of Islamic Art, Cairo.
    Carved wood, 12th century.*

207 Tunesien, Tunis, Dar Othman, Marmor,
    eingelegt, 17. Jh.
208 Indien, Agra, Tadsch Mahal, Marmor,
    eingelegt, 17. Jh.
209 Ägypten, Kairo, Islamisches Museum,
    Holz, geschnitzt, 12. Jh.

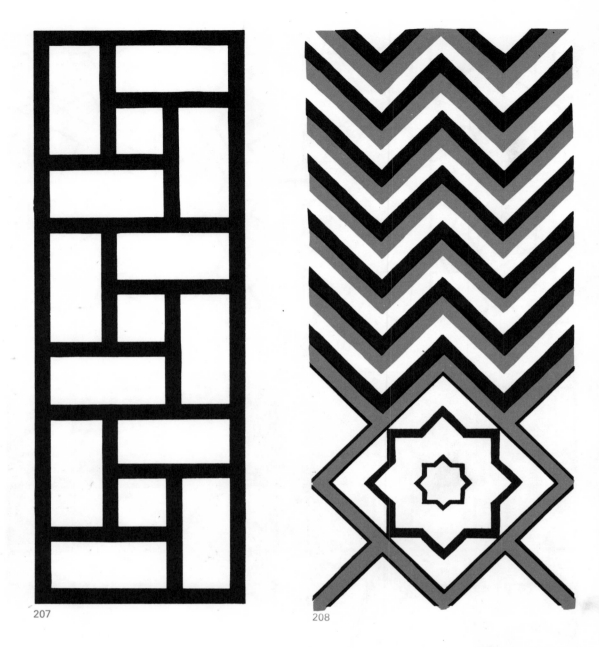

207

208

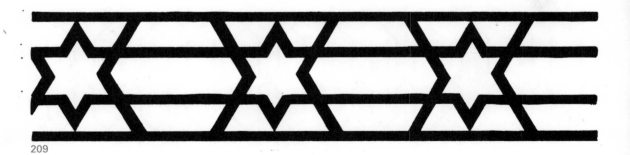

209

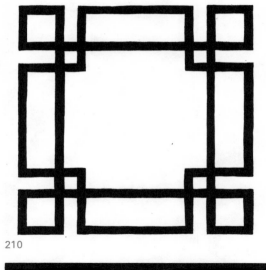

210

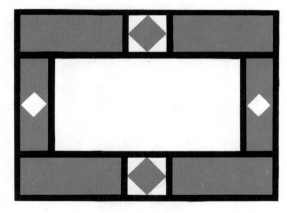

211

212

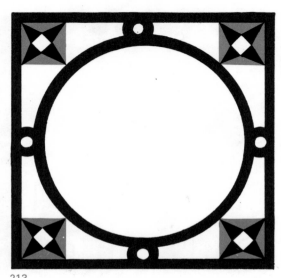

213

214

215

210 Egypte, Le Caire, palais de Radwan Bey, mosaïque de marbre, XVIIᵉ siècle.
211 Syrie, Damas, musée national, salle damascène, marbre incrusté, XVIIIᵉ siècle.
212 Syrie, Damas, musée national, salle damascène, marbre incrusté, XVIIIᵉ siècle.
213 Syrie, Damas, maison Sibai, marbre incrusté, XVIIIᵉ siècle.
214 Syrie, Damas, musée national, salle damascène, marbre incrusté, XVIIIᵉ siècle.
215 Syrie, Damas, musée national, salle damascène, marbre incrusté, XVIIIᵉ siècle.

210 Egypt: Cairo, Palace of Radwan Bey. Marble mosaic, 17th century.
211 Syria: National Museum, Damascus, Damascan Room. Inlaid marble, 18th century.
212 Syria: National Museum, Damascus, Damascan Room. Inlaid marble, 18th century.
213 Syria: Damascus, Sibai House. Inlaid marble, 18th century.
214 Syria: National Museum, Damascus, Damascan Room. Inlaid marble, 18th century.
215 Syria: National Museum, Damascus, Damascan Room. Inlaid marble, 18th century.

210 Ägypten, Kairo, Palast des Radwan Bey, Marmormosaik, 17. Jh.
211 Syrien, Damaskus, Nationalmuseum, Damaszenersaal, Marmor, eingelegt, 18. Jh.
212 Syrien, Damaskus, Nationalmuseum, Damaszenersaal, Marmor, eingelegt, 18. Jh.
213 Syrien, Damaskus, Haus Sibai, Marmor, eingelegt, 18. Jh.
214 Syrien, Damaskus, Nationalmuseum, Damaszenersaal, Marmor, eingelegt, 18. Jh.
215 Syrien, Damaskus, Nationalmuseum, Damaszenersaal, Marmor, eingelegt, 18. Jh.

216 Inde, Agra, mausolée d'Itimour ed-
Daula, marbre incrusté, XVIIᵉ siècle.
217 Egypte, Le Caire, médersa du sultan
Baybars, pierre sculptée, XIIIᵉ siècle.
218 Maroc, Meknès, broderie, XVIIIᵉ siècle.

216 *India: Agra, Mausoleum of Itimad al-
Dawla. Inlaid marble, 17th century.*
217 *Egypt: Cairo, Madrasah of Sultan Beybars. Carved stone, 13th century.*
218 *Morocco: Meknès. Embroidery, 18th
century.*

216 Indien, Agra, Mausoleum des Itimad ud-
Daula, Marmor, eingelegt, 17. Jh.
217 Ägypten, Kairo, Medrese des Sultans
Baibars, Stein, gehauen, 13. Jh.
218 Marokko, Meknes, Stickerei, 18. Jh.

216

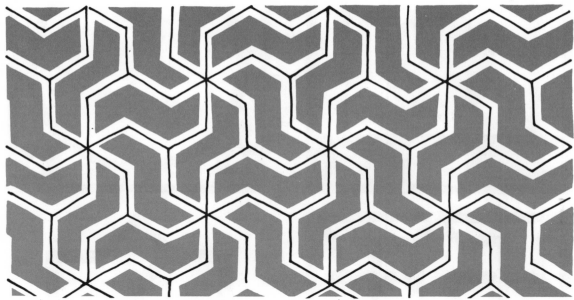

217

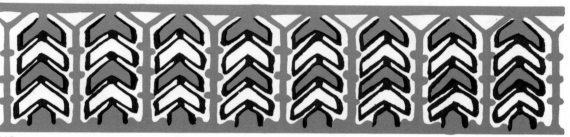

218

219

220

221

222

223 Algérie, Sedrata, plâtre sculpté, IXᵉ
siècle.
224 Algérie, Sedrata, plâtre sculpté, IXᵉ
siècle.
225 Maroc, Fès, mosaïque de faïence, XIVᵉ
siècle.

223 *Algeria: Sedrata. Stucco, 9th century.*
224 *Algeria: Sedrata. Stucco, 9th century.*
225 *Morocco: Fez. Tin-glazed earthenware*
mosaic, 14th century.

223 Algerien, Sedrata, Stuck, geschnitten,
9. Jh.
224 Algerien, Sedrata, Stuck, geschnitten,
9. Jh.
225 Marokko, Fez, Fayencemosaik, 14. Jh.

223

224

225

226

227

228

229

230 Egypte, Le Caire, musée arabe, bois
tourné, XIIᵉ siècle.
231 Maroc, Fès, médersa Bou Inaniya,
mosaïque de faïence, XIVᵉ siècle.
232 Perse, céramique, XVIIᵉ siècle.

230 *Egypt: Museum of Islamic Art, Cairo.*
Turned wood, 12th century.
231 *Morocco: Fez, Madrasah of Bu Inaniyya.*
Tin-glazed earthenware mosaic, 14th
century.
232 *Iran. Ceramic design, 17th century.*

230 Ägypten, Kairo, Islamisches Museum,
Holz, gedrechselt, 17. Jh.
231 Marokko, Fez, Medrese Bu Inaniya,
Fayencemosaik, 16. Jh.
232 Persien, Keramik, 17. Jh.

230

231

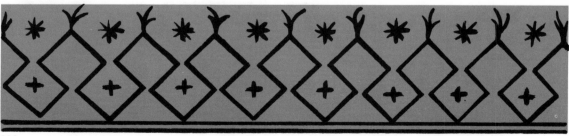

232

233

234

235

236 Egypte, Le Caire, bois tourné, XVᵉ siècle.
237 Turquie, galère impériale, nacre incrustée.
238 Egypte, Le Caire, Manzil al-Sinnari, bois sculpté, XVIIIᵉ siècle.
239 Egypte, Le Caire, Manzil al-Sinnari, bois sculpté, XVIIIᵉ siècle.

236 Egypt: Cairo. Turned wood, 15th century.
237 Turkey: imperial galley. Inlaid mother-of-pearl.
238 Egypt: Cairo, Beit (Manzil) Sennari. Carved wood, 18th century.
239 Egypt: Cairo, Beit (Manzil) Sennari. Carved wood, 18th century.

236 Ägypten, Kairo, Holz, gedrechselt, 15. Jh.
237 Türkei, kaiserliche Galeere, Perlmutt, eingelegt.
238 Ägypten, Kairo, Manzil al-Sinnari, Holz, geschnitzt, 18. Jh.
239 Ägypten, Kairo, Manzil al-Sinnari, Holz, geschnitzt, 18. Jh.

236

237

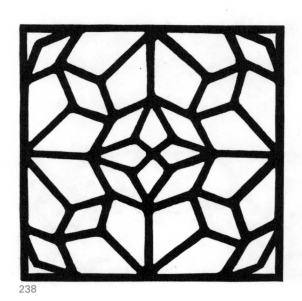

238   239

240 Maroc, Fès, mosaïque de faïence, XXᵉ siècle.

240 Morocco: Fez. Tin-glazed earthenware mosaic, 20th century.

240 Marokko, Fez, Fayencemosaik, 20. Jh.

241 Inde, Amber, ivoire incrusté.
242 Inde, Lahore, marbre incrusté, XVIIᵉ siècle.
243 Maroc, Taza, Grande Mosquée, plâtre sculpté et peint, XIIᵉ siècle.
244 Jérusalem, plâtre sculpté, VIIIᵉ siècle.

241 *India: Palace of Amber. Inlaid ivory.*
242 *India: Lahore. Inlaid marble, 17th century.*
243 *Morocco: Taza, Great Mosque. Painted plasterwork, 12th century.*
244 *Jerusalem. Stucco, 8th century.*

241 Indien, Amber, Elfenbein, eingelegt.
242 Indien, Lahore, Marmor, eingelegt, 17. Jh.
243 Marokko, Taza, Große Moschee, Stuck, geschnitten und bemalt, 12. Jh.
244 Jerusalem, Stuck, geschnitten, 8. Jh.

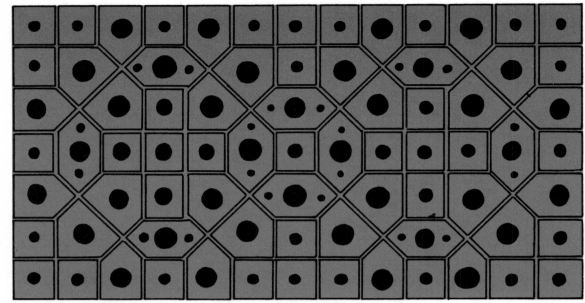

241

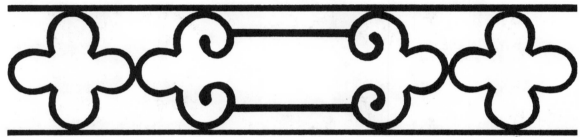

242

243

244

245

246

247

248

249

245 Egypte, Le Caire, musée arabe, bois sculpté, XIIe siècle.
246 Syrie, Damas, musée national, salle damascène, marbre incrusté, XVIIIe siècle.
247 Maroc, Tétouan, bois peint, XVIIIe siècle.
248 Transoxiane, Samarkand, céramique, VIIIe-IXe siècle.
249 Maroc, Fès, céramique.

245 *Egypt: Museum of Islamic Art, Cairo. Carved wood, 12th century.*
246 *Syria: National Museum, Damascus, Damascan Room. Inlaid marble, 18th century.*
247 *Morocco: Tetuan. Painted wood, 18th century.*
248 *Transoxiana: Samarkand. Ceramic design, 8th–9th century.*
249 *Morocco: Fez. Ceramic design.*

245 Ägypten, Kairo, Islamisches Museum, Holz, geschnitzt, 12. Jh.
246 Syrien, Damaskus, Nationalmuseum, Damaszenersaal, Marmor, eingelegt, 18. Jh.
247 Marokko, Tetuan, Holz, bemalt, 18. Jh.
248 Usbekische SSR, Sowjetunion, bis 16. Jh. Transoxanien, Samarkand, Keramik, 8.–9. Jh.
249 Marokko, Fez, Keramik.

250 Egypte, Le Caire, bois tourné, XVᵉ siècle.
251 Egypte, Le Caire, bois tourné, XVᵉ siècle.
252 Maroc, Fès, plâtre et faïence.

250 *Egypt: Cairo. Turned wood, 15th century.*
251 *Egypt: Cairo. Turned wood, 15th century.*
252 *Morocco: Fez. Plasterwork and tin-glazed earthenware.*

250 Ägypten, Kairo, Holz, gedrechselt, 15. Jh.
251 Ägypten, Kairo, Holz, gedrechselt, 15. Jh.
252 Marokko, Fez, Stuck und Fayence.

250

251

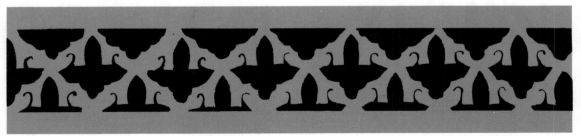

252

253

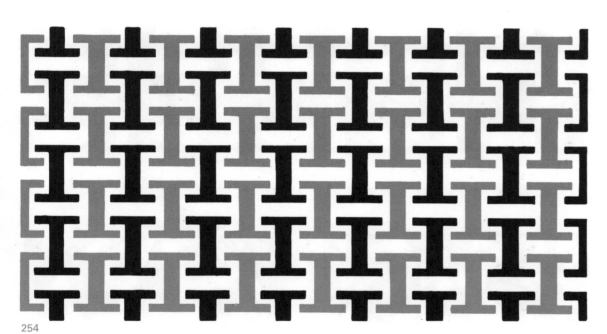

254

255

256 Maroc, Tétouan, jardin public, mosaïque de faïence, XXᵉ siècle.
257 Tunisie, Tunis, Dar Lajimi, mosaïque de faïence, XVIIᵉ siècle.
258 Turquie, Iznik, céramique, XVIᵉ siècle.
259 Maroc, Fès, mosaïque de faïence, XXᵉ siècle.
260 Turquie, Gebzé, bain de Çoban Moustafa Pacha, marbre incrusté.

256 *Morocco: Tetuan, public gardens. Tin-glazed earthenware mosaic, 20th century.*
257 *Tunisia: Tunis, Dar Lajimi. Tin-glazed earthenware mosaic, 17th century.*
258 *Turkey: Iznik. Ceramic design, 16th century.*
259 *Morocco: Fez. Tin-glazed earthenware mosaic, 20th century.*
260 *Turkey: Gebze, Bath of Çoban Mustapha Pasha. Inlaid marble.*

256 Marokko, Tetuan, öffentlicher Garten, Fayencemosaik, 20. Jh.
257 Tunesien, Tunis, Dar Lajimi, Fayencemosaik, 17. Jh.
258 Türkei, Iznik, Keramik, 16. Jh.
259 Marokko, Fez, Fayencemosaik, 20. Jh.
260 Türkei, Gebze, Bad des Tschoban Mustafa Pascha, Marmor, eingelegt.

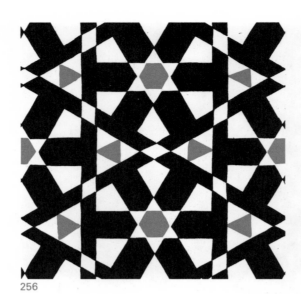

256

257

258

259

260

261

262

263

264

265

266 Tunisie, musée du Bardo, nacre incrustée, XVIIIᵉ-XIXᵉ siècle.
267 Espagne, Grenade, Alhambra, mosaïque de faïence, XIVᵉ siècle.
268 Turquie, broderie.

266 Tunisia: Bardo Museum, Tunis. Inlaid mother-of-pearl, 18th–19th century.
267 Spain: Granada, Alhambra Palace. Tinglazed earthenware mosaic, 14th century.
268 Turkey. Embroidery.

266 Tunesien, Nationalmuseum im Bardo, Perlmutt, eingelegt, 18.–19. Jh.
267 Spanien, Granada, Alhambra, Fayencemosaik, 14. Jh.
268 Türkei, Stickerei.

266

267

268

269

271

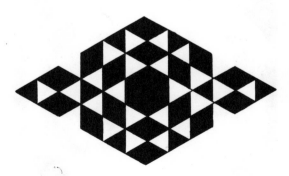

273

274

270

272

269 Maroc, Taza, Grande Mosquée, ivoire incrusté, XIIᵉ siècle.
270 Syrie, Damas, musée national, salle damascène, marbre incrusté, XVIIIᵉ siècle.
271 Egypte, Le Caire, palais de Radwan Bey, marbre incrusté, XVIIᵉ siècle.
272 Turquie, Gebzé, mosquée de Çoban Moustafa Pacha, marbre incrusté.
273 Maroc, Tétouan, jardin public, mosaïque de faïence, XXᵉ siècle.
274 Syrie, Damas, musée national, salle damascène, marbre incrusté, XVIIIᵉ siècle.

269 *Morocco: Taza, Great Mosque. Inlaid ivory, 12th century.*
270 *Syria: National Museum, Damascus, Damascan Room. Inlaid marble, 18th century.*
271 *Egypt: Cairo, Palace of Radwan Bey. Inlaid marble, 17th century.*
272 *Turkey: Gebze, Mosque of Çoban Mustapha Pasha. Inlaid marble.*
273 *Morocco: Tetuan, public gardens. Tinglazed earthenware mosaic, 20th century.*
274 *Syria: National Museum, Damascus, Damascan Room. Inlaid marble, 18th century.*

269 Marokko, Taza, Große Moschee, Elfenbein, eingelegt, 12. Jh.
270 Syrien, Damaskus, Nationalmuseum, Damaszenersaal, Marmor, eingelegt, 18. Jh.
271 Ägypten, Kairo, Palast des Radwan Bey, Marmor, eingelegt, 17. Jh.
272 Türkei, Gebze, Moschee des Tschoban Mustafa Pascha, Marmor, eingelegt.
273 Marokko, Tetuan, öffentlicher Garten, Fayencemosaik, 20. Jh.
274 Syrien, Damaskus, Nationalmuseum, Damaszenersaal, Marmor, eingelegt, 18. Jh.

275 Maroc, enluminure de Coran, XIXe
siècle.
276 Transoxiane, Samarkand, céramique,
VIIIe-IXe siècle.
277 Transoxiane, Samarkand, céramique,
VIIIe-IXe siècle.
278 Mésopotamie, céramique, IXe-Xe siècle.
279 Tunisie, Tunis, mosquée de la Zitouna,
marbre sculpté, IXe siècle.
280 Maroc, Fès, céramique.

275 *Morocco. Koran illumination, 19th century.*
276 *Transoxiana: Samarkand. Ceramic design, 8th–9th century.*
277 *Transoxiana: Samarkand. Ceramic design, 8th–9th century.*
278 *Mesopotamia. Ceramic design, 9th–10th century.*
279 *Tunisia: Tunis, Zitouna Mosque. Carved marble, 9th century.*
280 *Morocco: Fez. Ceramic design.*

275 Marokko, Miniatur zum Koran, 19. Jh.
276 Usbekische SSR, Sowjetunion, bis
16. Jh. Transoxanien, Samarkand, Keramik, 8.–9. Jh.
277 Usbekische SSR, Sowjetunion, bis
16. Jh. Transoxanien, Samarkand, Keramik, 8.–9. Jh.
278 Mesopotamien, Keramik, 9.–10. Jh.
279 Tunesien, Tunis, Moschee az-Zeituna,
Marmor, behauen, 9. Jh.
280 Marokko, Fez, Keramik.

275

276

277

278

279

280

281

282

283

284

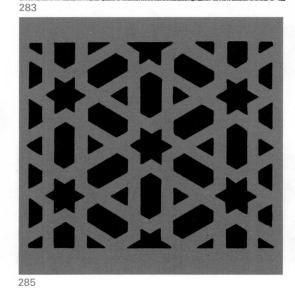

285

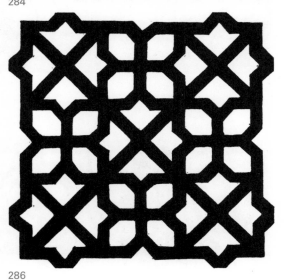

286

281 Maroc, bois sculpté.
282 Maroc, argent gravé.
283 Egypte, bois sculpté, XVᵉ siècle.
284 Iran, Ispahan, mosquée du Vendredi, mosaïque de faïence, XVᵉ siècle.
285 Egypte, Le Caire, musée arabe, bois sculpté, XIIᵉ siècle.
286 Inde, Fathepour Sikri, Djami Masdjid, claustra de marbre, XVIᵉ siècle.

281 *Morocco. Carved wood.*
282 *Morocco. Engraved silver.*
283 *Egypt. Carved wood, 15th century.*
284 *Iran: Isfahan, Friday Mosque. Tin-glazed earthenware mosaic, 15th century.*
285 *Egypt: Museum of Islamic Art, Cairo. Carved wood, 12th century.*
286 *India: Fatehpur Sikri, Great Mosque. Marble tracery window, 16th century.*

281 Marokko, Holz, geschnitzt.
282 Marokko, Silber, graviert.
283 Ägypten, Holz, geschnitzt, 15. Jh.
284 Iran, Isfahan, Große Freitagsmoschee, Fayencemosaik, 15. Jh.
285 Ägypten, Kairo, Islamisches Museum, Holz, geschnitzt, 12. Jh.
286 Indien, Fathepur Sikri, Große Moschee, Marmor, durchbrochen gearbeitet, 16. Jh.

287 Maroc, Fès el-Bali, fer forgé, XXᵉ siècle.
288 Maroc, Fès el-Bali, fer forgé, XXᵉ siècle.
289 Mésopotamie, Samarra, plâtre, IXᵉ siècle.

287 *Morocco: Fes al-Bali. Wrought iron, 20th century.*
288 *Morocco: Fes al-Bali. Wrought iron, 20th century.*
289 *Iraq: Samarra. Plasterwork, 9th century.*

287 Marokko, Fez al-Bali, Schmiedeeisen, 20. Jh.
288 Marokko, Fez al-Bali, Schmiedeeisen, 20. Jh.
289 Mesopotamien, Samarra, Stuck, 9. Jh.

287

288

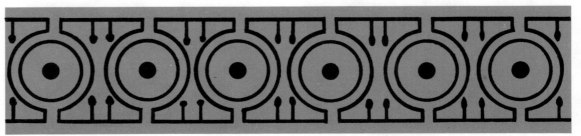

289

290

291

292

293

294

295

296 Maroc, Fès, mosaïque de faïence, XXᵉ
siècle.
297 Maroc, Fès, mosaïque de faïence, XIVᵉ
siècle.
298 Turquie, broderie.

296 *Morocco: Fez. Tin-glazed earthenware
mosaic, 20th century.*
297 *Morocco: Fez. Tin-glazed earthenware
mosaic, 14th century.*
298 *Turkey. Embroidery.*

296 Marokko, Fez, Fayencemosaik, 20. Jh.
297 Marokko, Fez, Fayencemosaik, 14. Jh.
298 Türkei, Stickerei.

296

297

298

299

299 Maroc, Fès, médersa Bou Inaniya, mosaïque de faïence, XIVᵉ siècle.
300 Turquie, Edirné, mosquée de Sélimiyé, marbre sculpté, XVIᵉ siècle.
301 Jérusalem, marbre sculpté, VIIᵉ-VIIIᵉ siècle.
302 Maroc, Télouet, palais du Glaoui, bois ajusté, XIXᵉ siècle.

299 *Morocco: Fez, Madrasah of Bu Inaniyya. Tin-glazed earthenware mosaic, 14th century.*
300 *Turkey: Edirne, Mosque of Sultan Selim. Carved marble, 16th century.*
301 *Jerusalem. Carved marble, 7th–8th century.*
302 *Morocco: Telouet, Glawa Palace. Joined wood, 19th century.*

299 Marokko, Fez, Medrese Bu Inaniya, Fayencemosaik, 14. Jh.
300 Türkei, Edirne, Selimiye, Marmor, behauen, 16. Jh.
301 Jerusalem, Marmor, behauen, 7.—8. Jh.
302 Marokko, Teluet, Palast des Glawi, Holz, eingepaßt, 19. Jh.

300

301

302

303

304

305

306

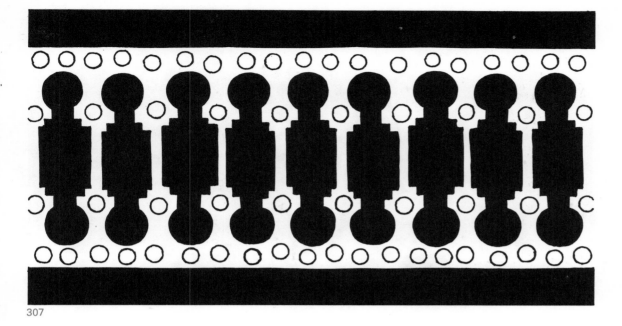

307

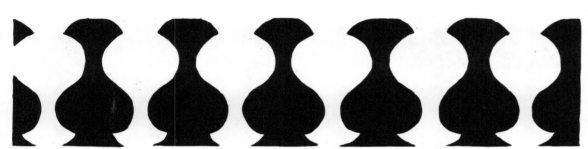

308

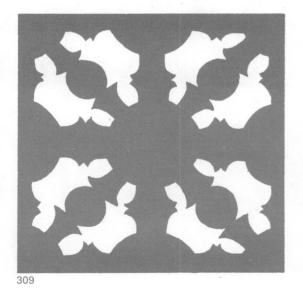

309

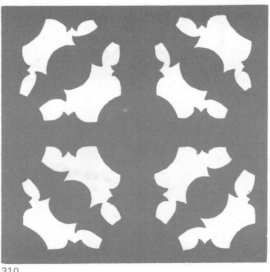

310

307 Maroc, Télouet, palais du Glaoui, bois ajusté, XIXᵉ siècle.
308 Syrie, Damas, mosquée des Omeyyades, marbre incrusté.
309 Syrie, Damas, musée des Arts et Traditions populaires, bois tourné.
310 Syrie, Damas, musée des Arts et Traditions populaires, bois tourné.

307 Morocco: Telouet, Glawa Palace. Joined wood, 19th century.
308 Syria: Damascus, Umayyad Mosque. Inlaid marble.
309 Syria: Museum of Folk Art, Damascus. Turned wood.
310 Syria: Museum of Folk Art, Damascus. Turned wood.

307 Marokko, Teluet, Palast des Glawi, Holz, eingepaßt, 19. Jh.
308 Syrien, Damaskus, Omaijadenmoschee, Marmor, eingelegt.
309 Syrien, Damaskus, Museum volkstümlicher Kunst, Holz, gedrechselt.
310 Syrien, Damaskus, Museum volkstümlicher Kunst, Holz, gedrechselt.

311 Maroc, Fès, mosaïque de faïence. XXe
siècle.
312 Espagne, Grenade, Alhambra, mosaïque de faïence, XIe siècle.
313 Perse, verre peint, XIIIe siècle.

311 *Morocco: Fez. Tin-glazed earthenware
mosaic, 20th century.*
312 *Spain: Granada, Alhambra Palace. Tin-
glazed earthenware mosaic, 11th century.*
313 *Iran. Painted glass, 13th century.*

311 Marokko, Fez, Fayencemosaik, 20. Jh.
312 Spanien, Granada, Alhambra, Fayencemosaik, 11. Jh.
313 Persien, Glas, bemalt, 13. Jh.

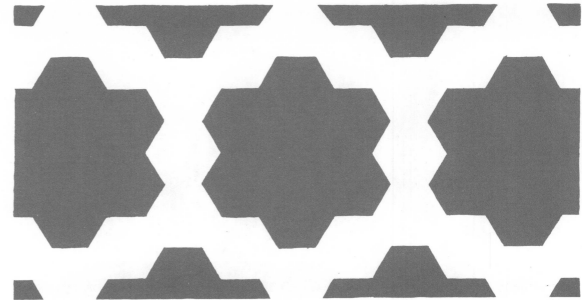

311

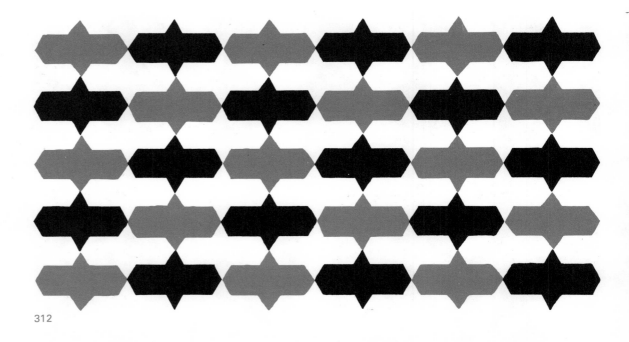

312

313

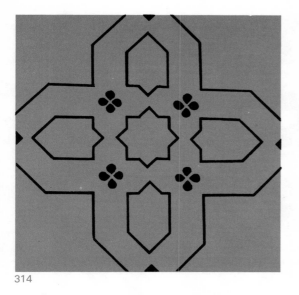

314

315

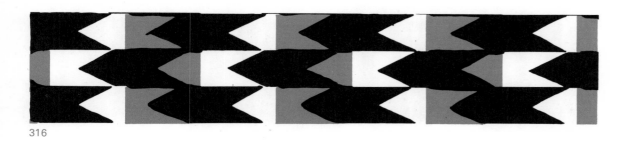

316

317

318

319

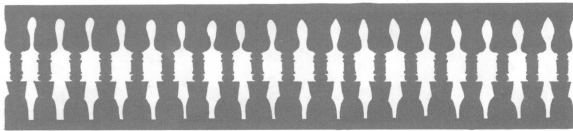

320

321

322

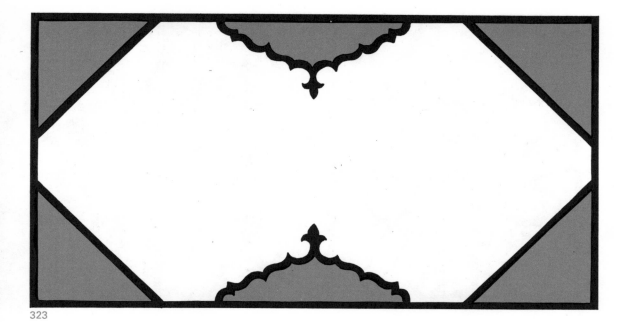

323

324

325

326

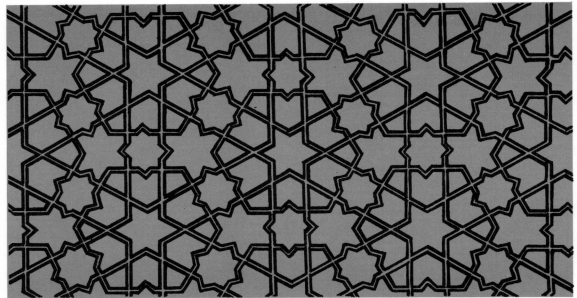

327

328

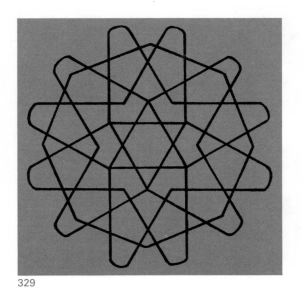

329

330

331

332

333

334

331 Egypte, Le Caire, bois tourné, XVᵉ siècle.
332 Turquie, broderie.
333 Tunisie, Tunis, Dar el-Bey, pierre incrustée, XVIIᵉ siècle.
334 Egypte, Le Caire, mausolée Barkouk, bois sculpté, XIVᵉ siècle.

331 Egypt: Cairo. Turned wood, 15th century.
332 Turkey. Embroidery.
333 Tunisia: Tunis, Dar el-Bey. Inlaid stone, 17th century.
334 Egypt: Cairo, Barquq Mausoleum. Carved wood, 14th century.

331 Ägypten, Kairo, Holz, gedrechselt, 15. Jh.
332 Türkei, Stickerei.
333 Tunesien, Tunis, Dar al-Bey, Stein, eingelegt, 17. Jh.
334 Ägypten, Kairo, Mausoleum des Barquq, Holz, geschnitzt, 14. Jh.

335 Turquie, marbre incrusté.
336 Turquie, ornementation.
337 Maroc, Fès, médersa Bou Inaniya, mosaïque de faïence, XIVᵉ siècle.
338 Maroc, Fès, médersa Bou Inaniya, mosaïque de faïence, XIVᵉ siècle.
339 Egypte, Le Caire, mausolée du sultan Kaït Bey, mosaïque de marbre, XVᵉ siècle.

335 Turkey. Inlaid marble.
336 Turkey. Ornamentation.
337 Morocco: Fez. Madrasah of Bu Inaniyya. Tin-glazed earthenware mosaic, 14th century.
338 Morocco: Fez, Madrasah of Bu Inaniyya. Tin-glazed earthenware mosaic, 14th century.
339 Egypt: Cairo, Mausoleum of Qait Bey. Marble mosaic, 15th century.

335 Türkei, Marmor, eingelegt.
336 Türkei, Ornament.
337 Marokko, Fez, Medrese Bu Inaniya, Fayencemosaik, 14. Jh.
338 Marokko, Fez, Medrese Bu Inaniya, Fayencemosaik, 14. Jh.
339 Ägypten, Kairo, Mausoleum des Qait Bey, Marmormosaik, 15. Jh.

335

336

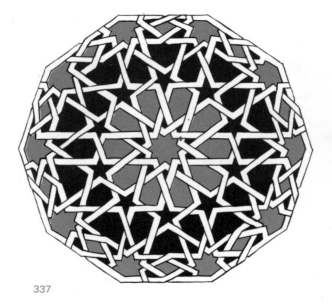

337

338

339

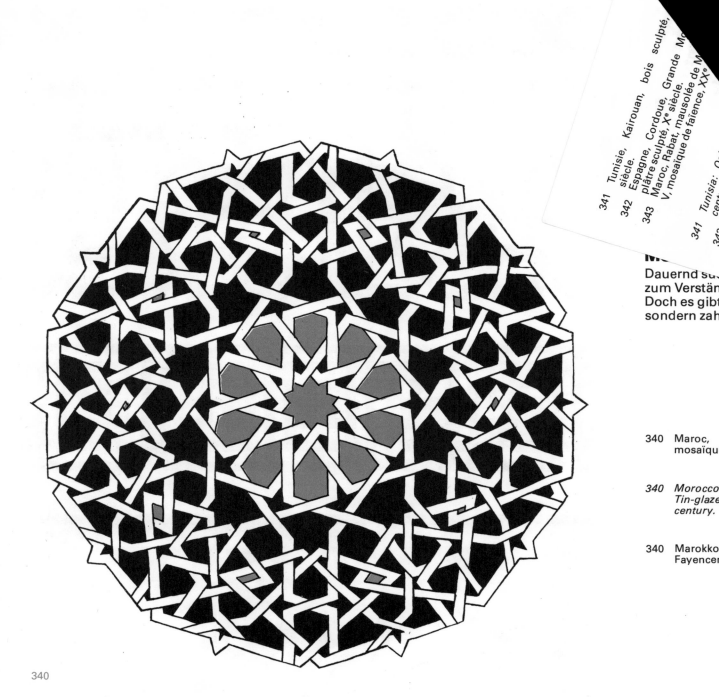

M
Dauernd su
zum Verständnis.
Doch es gibt nicht nur ein
sondern zahlreiche.

340 Maroc, Fès, médersa Bou Inaniya, mosaïque de faïence, XIVe siècle.

340 Morocco: Fez, Madrasah of Bu Inaniyya. Tin-glazed earthenware mosaic, 14th century.

340 Marokko, Fez, Medrese Bu Inaniya, Fayencemosaik, 14. Jh.

340

IXe

osquée,

ohammed
siècle.

arved wood, 9th

eat Mosque. Stucco,

t, Mausoleum of Mu-
n-glazed earthenware mo-
tury.

en, Kairuan, Holz, geschnitzt,

nien, Cordoba, Große Moschee,
uck, geschnitten, 10. Jh.
Marokko, Rabat, Mausoleum Mohammeds V., Fayencemosaik, 20. Jh.

341

342

343

344

345

346

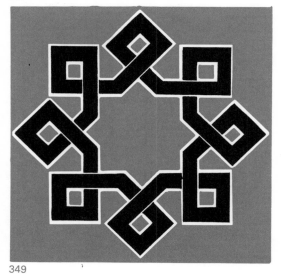

347

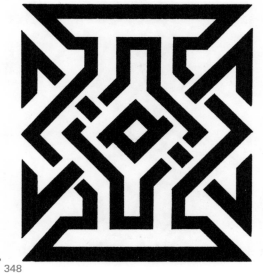

348

349

344 Egypte, Le Caire, bois sculpté, XIIᵉ siècle.
345 Syrie, enluminure de Coran, IXᵉ siècle.
346 Egypte, Le Caire, musée arabe, bois sculpté, VIIᵉ siècle.
347 Jérusalem, pierre sculptée, IXᵉ siècle.
348 Syrie, Damas, médersa az-Zahiriyya, marbre incrusté, XIIIᵉ siècle.
349 Tunisie, Tunis, Dar Othman, plâtre sculpté, XVIIᵉ siècle.

344 Egypt: Cairo. Carved wood, 12th century.
345 Syria. Koran illumination, 9th century.
346 Egypt: Museum of Islamic Art, Cairo. Carved wood, 7th century.
347 Jerusalem. Carved stone, 9th century.
348 Syria: Damascus, Madrasah of al-Zahiriyya. Inlaid marble, 13th century.
349 Tunisia: Tunis, Dar Othman. Stucco, 17th century.

344 Ägypten, Kairo, Holz, geschnitzt, 12. Jh.
345 Syrien, Miniatur zum Koran, 9. Jh.
346 Ägypten, Kairo, Islamisches Museum, Holz, geschnitzt, 7. Jh.
347 Jerusalem, Stein, behauen, 9. Jh.
348 Syrien, Damaskus, Medrese az-Zahiriyya, Marmor, eingelegt, 13. Jh.
349 Tunesien, Tunis, Dar Othman, Stuck, geschnitten, 17. Jh.

350 Tunisie, Kairouan, Grande Mosquée, bois sculpté, XIe siècle.
351 Egypte, Le Caire, musée arabe, bois sculpté, IXe siècle.
352 Maroc, Rabat, mausolée de Mohammed V, mosaïque de faïence, XXe siècle.
353 Tunisie, Sfax, Grande Mosquée, bois sculpté, IXe siècle.

350 *Tunisia: Qairawan, Great Mosque. Carved wood, 11th century.*
351 *Egypt: Museum of Islamic Art, Cairo. Carved wood, 9th century.*
352 *Morocco: Rabat, Mausoleum of Muhammad V. Tin-glazed earthenware mosaic, 20th century.*
353 *Tunisia: Sfax, Great Mosque. Carved wood, 9th century.*

350 Tunesien, Kairuan, Große Moschee, Holz, geschnitzt, 11. Jh.
351 Ägypten, Kairo, Islamisches Museum, Holz, geschnitzt, 9. Jh.
352 Marokko, Rabat, Mausoleum Mohammeds V., Fayencemosaik, 20. Jh.
353 Tunesien, Sfax, Große Moschee, Holz, geschnitzt, 9. Jh.

350

351

352

353

354

355

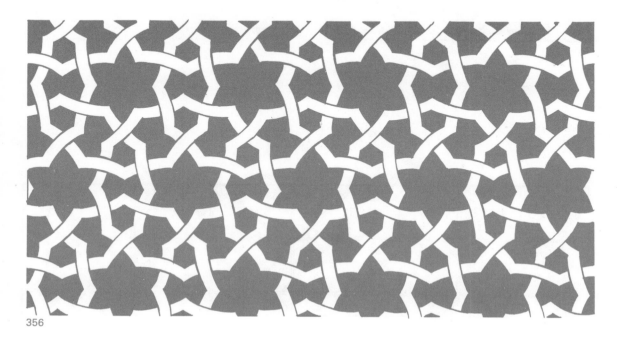

356

354 Syrie, Damas, mosquée des Omeyyades, marbre sculpté, VIIIᵉ siècle.
355 Maroc, Fès, médersa el-Attarin, mosaïque de faïence, XIVᵉ siècle.
356 Egypte, Le Caire, mosquée el-Azhar, plâtre sculpté, Xᵉ siècle.

354 *Syria: Damascus, Umayyad Mosque. Carved marble, 8th century.*
355 *Morocco: Fez, Madrasah of al-Attarin. Tin-glazed earthenware mosaic, 14th century.*
356 *Egypt: Cairo, Mosque of al-Azhar. Stucco, 10th century.*

354 Syrien, Damaskus, Omaijadenmoschee, Marmor, behauen, 8. Jh.
355 Marokko, Fez, Medrese al-Attarin, Fayencemosaik, 14. Jh.
356 Ägypten, Kairo, Moschee al-Azhar, Stuck, geschnitten, 10. Jh.

357 Syrie, Qasr al-Hair al-Gharbi, plâtre
   sculpté, VIIIe siècle.
358 Turquie, ornementation.
359 Maroc, Fès, médersa Bou Inaniya,
   mosaïque de faïence, XIVe siècle.
360 Turquie, marbre incrusté.
361 Algérie, Tlemcen, plâtre sculpté, XIVe
   siècle.

357 *Syria: Qasr al-Hair al-Gharbi. Stucco,*
   8th century.
358 *Turkey. Ornamentation.*
359 *Morocco: Fez, Madrasah of Bu Inaniyya.*
   Tin-glazed earthenware mosaic, 14th
   century.
360 *Turkey. Inlaid marble.*
361 *Algeria: Tlemcen. Stucco, 14th century.*

357 Syrien, Qasr al-Hair al-Gharbi, Stuck,
   geschnitten, 8. Jh.
358 Türkei, Ornament.
359 Marokko, Fez, Medrese Bu Inaniya,
   Fayencemosaik, 14. Jh.
360 Türkei, Marmor, eingelegt.
361 Algerien, Tlemcen, Stuck, geschnitten,
   14. Jh.

357

358

359

360

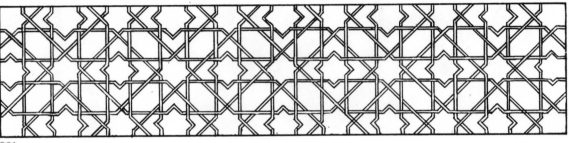

361

104   **357-361**

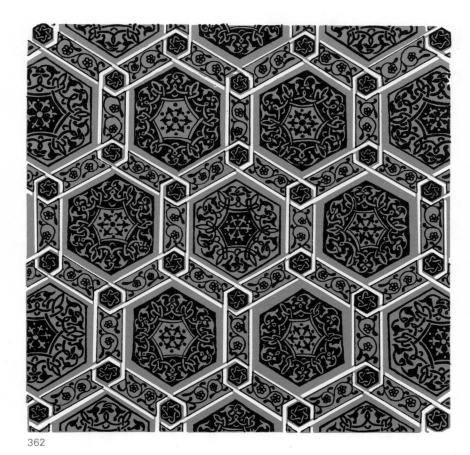

362

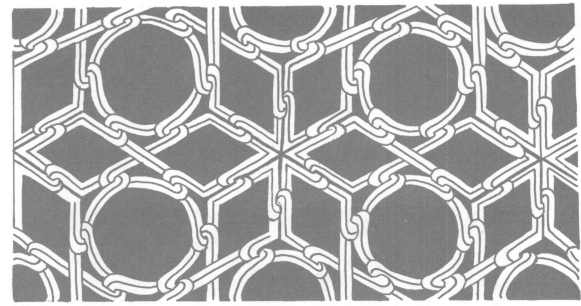

363

364

365

366

367

368

369

370

371

367 Algérie, Alger, Grande Mosquée, bois sculpté, XIᵉ siècle.
368 Tunisie, Kairouan, Grande Mosquée, bois sculpté, XIᵉ siècle.
369 Egypte, Le Caire, Mosquée Ibn Touloun, plâtre sculpté, IXᵉ siècle.
370 Espagne, Grenade, Alhambra, mosaïque de faïence, XIVᵉ-XVᵉ siècle.
371 Maroc, Rabat, porte des Oudaïa, pierre sculptée, XIIᵉ siècle.

367 *Algeria: Algiers, Great Mosque. Carved wood, 11th century.*
368 *Tunisia: Qairawan, Great Mosque. Carved wood, 11th century.*
369 *Egypt: Cairo, Mosque of Ibn Tulun. Stucco, 9th century.*
370 *Spain: Granada, Alhambra Palace. Tin-glazed earthenware mosaic, 14th–15th century.*
371 *Morocco: Rabat, Oudaia Gate. Carved stone, 12th century.*

367 Algerien, Algier, Große Moschee, Holz, geschnitzt, 11. Jh.
368 Tunesien, Kairuan, Große Moschee, Holz, geschnitzt, 11. Jh.
369 Ägypten, Kairo, Moschee des Ibn Tulun, Stuck, geschnitten, 9. Jh.
370 Spanien, Granada, Alhambra, Fayence-mosaik, 14.–15. Jh.
371 Marokko, Rabat, Tor der Oudaias, Stein, behauen, 12. Jh.

372 Egypte, Le Caire, mosquée Hassan,
marbre incrusté, XIVᵉ siècle.
373 Egypte, Le Caire, mosquée Hassan,
marbre incrusté, XIVᵉ siècle.
374 Maroc, Fès, sanctuaire d'Idris II, mosaïque de faïence, XVIIIᵉ siècle.
375 Egypte, Le Caire, mosquée d'el-Achraf
Barsebai, mosaïque de marbre, XVᵉ
siècle.

372 *Egypt: Cairo, Mosque of Sultan Hassan.*
Inlaid marble, 14th century.
373 *Egypt: Cairo, Mosque of Sultan Hassan.*
Inlaid marble, 14th century.
374 *Morocco: Fez, Sanctuary of Idriss II. Tin-*
glazed earthenware mosaic, 8th century.
375 *Egypt: Cairo, Mosque of al-Ashraf Bar-*
sebai. Marble mosaic, 15th century.

372 Ägypten, Kairo, Moschee des Hassan,
Marmor, eingelegt, 14. Jh.
373 Ägypten, Kairo, Moschee des Hassan,
Marmor, eingelegt, 14. Jh.
374 Marokko, Fez, Mausoleum des Idris II.,
Fayencemosaik, 18. Jh.
375 Ägypten, Kairo, Moschee des al-Aschraf
Barsbey, Marmormosaik, 15. Jh.

373

374

372

375

376

377

378

379

380 Tunisie, Kairouan, Grande Mosquée,
 bois sculpté, XIᵉ siècle.
381 Tunisie, Tunis, Sidi Qasim el-Jalizi,
 plâtre sculpté, XIVᵉ siècle.
382 Algérie, Tlemcen, mosquée Sidi Bou
 Médine, plâtre sculpté, XIVᵉ siècle.

380 *Tunisia: Qairawan, Great Mosque.*
 Carved wood, 11th century.
381 *Tunisia: Tunis, Sidi Qasim el-Jalizi.*
 Stucco, 14th century.
382 *Algeria: Tlemcen, Mosque of Sidi Bu*
 Medina. Stucco, 14th century.

380 Tunesien, Kairuan, Große Moschee,
 Holz, geschnitzt, 11. Jh.
381 Tunesien, Tunis, Sidi Qasim al-Jalizi,
 Stuck, geschnitten, 14. Jh.
382 Algerien, Tlemcen, Moschee von Bu
 Medine, Stuck, geschnitten, 14. Jh.

380

381

382

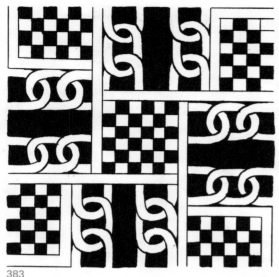

383

384

385

386

387

388

383 Perse, céramique, Xᵉ siècle.
384 Espagne, Burgos, plâtre sculpté.
385 Perse, céramique, Xᵉ siècle.
386 Maroc, céramique.
387 Syrie, Damas, mosquée des Omeyyades, plâtre sculpté.
388 Perse, faïence, XIIIᵉ siècle.

383 Iran. Ceramic design, 10th century.
384 Spain: Burgos. Stucco.
385 Iran. Ceramic design, 10th century.
386 Morocco. Ceramic design.
387 Syria: Damascus, Umayyad Mosque. Stucco.
388 Iran. Tin-glazed earthenware, 13th century.

383 Persien, Keramik, 10. Jh.
384 Spanien, Burgos, Stuck, geschnitten.
385 Persien, Keramik, 10. Jh.
386 Marokko, Keramik.
387 Syrien, Damaskus, Omaijadenmoschee, Stuck, geschnitten.
388 Persien, Fayence, 13. Jh.

389 Maroc, Tétouan, carreaux de faïence,
XXᵉ siècle.
390 Espagne, Cordoue, chapelle royale,
mosaïque de faïence, XIVᵉ siècle.
391 Tunisie, Gabès, médersa Mouradiya,
marbre incrusté, XVIIᵉ siècle.
392 Maroc, Rabat, mausolée de Mohammed
V, mosaïque de faïence XXᵉ siècle.

389 *Morocco: Tetuan. Tin-glazed earthenware tiles, 20th century.*
390 *Spain: Cordoba, royal chapel. Tin-glazed earthenware mosaic, 14th century.*
391 *Tunisia: Gabès, Mouradiya Madrasah.
Inlaid marble, 17th century.*
392 *Morocco: Rabat, Mausoleum of
Muhammad V. Tin-glazed earthenware
mosaic, 20th century.*

389 Marokko, Tetuan, Fayencefliesen,
20. Jh.
390 Spanien, Cordoba, königliche Kapelle,
Fayencemosaik, 14. Jh.
391 Tunesien, Gabes, Muradiya-Medrese,
Marmor, eingelegt, 17. Jh.
392 Marokko, Rabat, Mausoleum Mohammeds V., Fayencemosaik, 20. Jh.

389

390

391

392

393

394

395

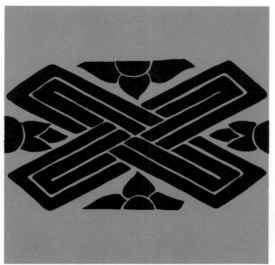

396

393 Egypte, Le Caire, mausolée du sultan Kaloun, plâtre sculpté, XIIIᵉ siècle.
394 Espagne, Grenade, Alhambra, plâtre sculpté, XIVᵉ siècle.
395 Turquie, Gebzé, bain de Çoban Moustafa Pacha, marbre incrusté.
396 Egypte, Le Caire, musée arabe, bois sculpté, VIIIᵉ siècle.

393 Egypt: Cairo, Mausoleum of Sultan Qala-un. Stucco, 13th century.
394 Spain: Granada, Alhambra Palace. Stucco, 14th century.
395 Turkey: Gebze, Bath of Çoban Mustapha Pasha. Inlaid marble.
396 Egypt: Museum of Islamic Art, Cairo. Carved wood, 8th century.

393 Ägypten, Kairo, Mausoleum des Sultans Qalaun, Stuck, geschnitten, 13. Jh.
394 Spanien, Granada, Alhambra, Stuck, geschnitten, 14. Jh.
395 Türkei, Gebze, Bad des Tschoban Mustafa Pascha, Marmor, eingelegt.
396 Ägypten, Kairo, Islamisches Museum, Holz, geschnitzt, 8. Jh.

397 Syrie, Alep, marbre incrusté, XIIIe siècle.
398 Egypte, Le Caire, mosquée Ibn Touloun, plâtre sculpté, IXe siècle.
399 Maroc, Fès, bois sculpté.
400 Maroc, Rabat, musée des Oudaïa, bois sculpté et peint.

397 Syria: Aleppo. Inlaid marble, 13th century.
398 Egypt: Cairo, Mosque of Ibn Tulun. Stucco, 9th century.
399 Morocco: Fez. Carved wood.
400 Morocco: Rabat, Oudaia Museum. Carved and painted wood.

397 Syrien, Aleppo, Marmor, eingelegt, 13. Jh.
398 Ägypten, Kairo, Moschee des Ibn Tulun, Stuck, geschnitten, 9. Jh.
399 Marokko, Fez, Holz, geschnitzt.
400 Marokko, Rabat, Museum der Oudaias, Holz, geschnitzt und bemalt.

397

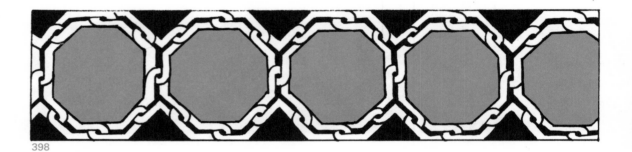

398

399

400

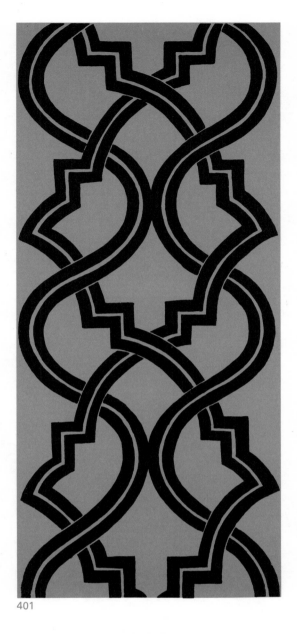

401

402

401 Tunisie, Tunis, Dar Lajimi, plâtre sculpté, XVIIᵉ siècle.
402 Tunisie, Tunis, Dar Lajimi, plâtre sculpté, XVIIᵉ siècle.
403 Espagne, Grenade, Alhambra, bois sculpté, XIVᵉ siècle.

401 Tunisia: Tunis, Dar Lajimi. Stucco, 17th century.
402 Tunisia: Tunis, Dar Lajimi. Stucco, 17th century.
403 Spain: Granada, Alhambra Palace. Carved wood, 14th century.

401 Tunesien, Tunis, Dar Lajimi, Stuck, geschnitten, 17. Jh.
402 Tunesien, Tunis, Dar Lajimi, Stuck, geschnitten, 17. Jh.
403 Spanien, Granada, Alhambra, Holz, geschnitten, 14. Jh.

403

404 Egypte, Le Caire, mosquée Ibn Touloun, plâtre sculpté, IXᵉ siècle.
405 Maroc, Fès, médersa es-Sahrij, plâtre sculpté, XIVᵉ siècle.
406 Maroc, Fès, sanctuaire d'Idris II, plâtre sculpté, XVIIIᵉ siècle.
407 Espagne, Cordoue, pierre sculptée, Xᵉ siècle.
408 Syrie, Damas, mosquée des Omeyyades, plâtre sculpté.
409 Maroc, Fès, médersa Bou Inaniya, bois sculpté, XIVᵉ siècle.

404 Egypt: Cairo, Mosque of Ibn Tulun. Stucco, 9th century.
405 Morocco: Fez, Madrasah of al-Sahridj. Stucco, 14th century.
406 Morocco: Fez, Sanctuary of Idriss II. Stucco, 18th century.
407 Spain: Cordoba. Carved stone, 10th century.
408 Syria: Damascus, Umayyad Mosque. Stucco.
409 Morocco: Fez, Madrasah of Bu Inaniyya. Carved wood, 14th century.

404 Ägypten, Kairo, Moschee des Ibn Tulun, Stuck, geschnitten, 9. Jh.
405 Marokko, Fez, Medrese as-Sahrij, Stuck, geschnitten, 14. Jh.
406 Marokko, Fez, Mausoleum des Idris II., Stuck, geschnitten, 18. Jh.
407 Spanien, Cordoba, Stein, behauen, 10. Jh.
408 Syrien, Damaskus, Omaijadenmoschee, Stuck, geschnitten.
409 Marokko, Fez, Medrese Bu Inaniya, Holz, geschnitzt, 14. Jh.

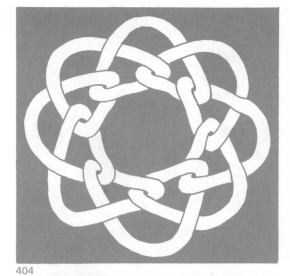

404

405

406

407

408

409

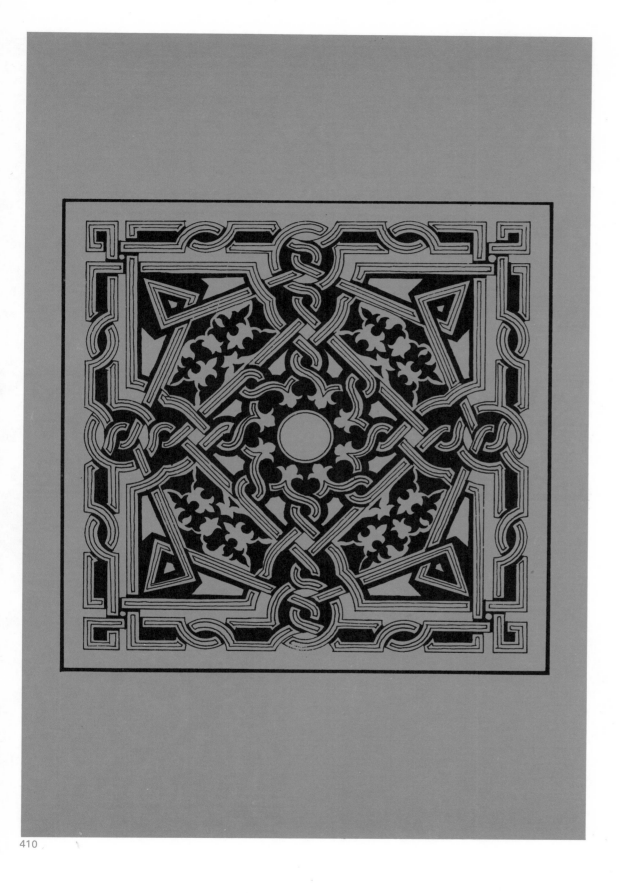

410

410

410 Syrie, Damas, mosquée d'er-Rifai, marbre incrusté.

410 Syria: Damascus, Mosque of al-Rifai. Inlaid marble.

410 Syrien, Damaskus, Moschee des ar-Rifai, Marmor, eingelegt.

410 **117**

411 Egypte, Le Caire, mosquée d'Ibn Touloun, claustra de plâtre sculpté, IXe
siècle.
412 Egypte (?), marbre incrusté, XIVe siècle.
413 Espagne, Saragosse, Aljaféria, plâtre
sculpté, XIe siècle.
414 Egypte, Le Caire, mosquée Ibn Touloun,
claustra de plâtre sculpté, IXe siècle.

411 *Egypt: Cairo, Mosque of Ibn Tulun.*
Stucco tracery window, 9th century.
412 *Egypt (?). Inlaid marble, 14th century.*
413 *Spain: Saragossa, Aljaferia Palace.*
Stucco, 11th century.
414 *Egypt: Cairo, Mosque of Ibn Tulun.*
Stucco tracery window, 9th century.

411 Ägypten, Kairo, Moschee des Ibn Tulun,
Fenstergitter, Stuck, geschnitten, 9. Jh.
412 Ägypten, (?), Marmor, eingelegt, 14. Jh.
413 Spanien, Zaragoza, Aljaferia, Stuck, geschnitten, 11. Jh.
414 Ägypten, Kairo, Moschee des Ibn Tulun,
Fenstergitter, Stuck, geschnitten, 9. Jh.

411

412

413

414

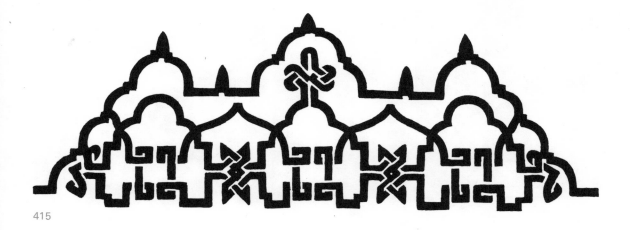

415

416

417

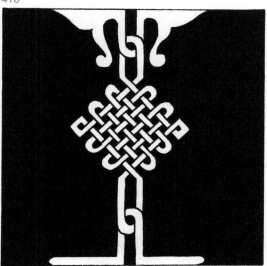

418

419

420

421

422

423

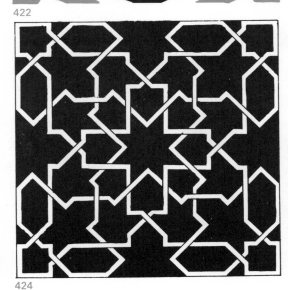

424

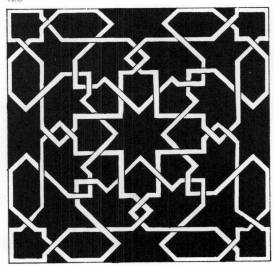

425

426

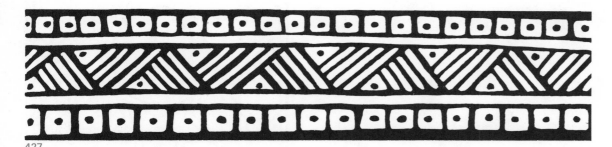

427

428

429

430 Egypte, Le Caire, marbre incrusté, XVe siècle.
431 Tunisie, Tunis, Dar el-Mrabet, bois sculpté et peint, XVIIe siècle.
432 Egypte, Le Caire, musée arabe, bois sculpté, XIe siècle.

430 Egypt: Cairo. Inlaid marble, 15th century.
431 Tunisia: Tunis, Dar el-Mrabet. Carved and painted wood, 17th century.
432 Egypt: Museum of Islamic Art, Cairo. Carved wood, 11th century.

430 Ägypten, Kairo, Marmor, eingelegt, 15. Jh.
431 Tunesien, Tunis, Dar al-Mrabet, Holz, geschnitzt und bemalt, 17. Jh.
432 Ägypten, Kairo, Islamisches Museum, Holz, geschnitzt, 11. Jh.

430

431

432

433

434

435

436

437

438

433 Egypte, Le Caire, mosquée Ibn Touloun, plâtre sculpté, IXe siècle.
434 Maroc, cuivre, XVIIIe siècle.
435 Egypte, Le Caire, mosquée Ibn Touloun, plâtre sculpté, IXe siècle.
436 Syrie, céramique, XVIIe siècle.
437 Perse, Rai, céramique, VIIIe siècle.
438 Perse, Kashan, céramique, XIIIe siècle.

433 Egypt: Cairo, Mosque of Ibn Tulun. Stucco, 9th century.
434 Morocco. Copper, 18th century.
435 Egypt: Cairo, Mosque of Ibn Tulun. Stucco, 9th century.
436 Syria. Ceramic design. 17th century.
437 Iran: Rayy. Ceramic design, 8th century.
438 Iran: Kashan. Ceramic design, 13th century.

433 Ägypten, Kairo, Moschee des Ibn Tulun, Stuck, geschnitten, 9. Jh.
434 Marokko, Kupfer, 18. Jh.
435 Ägypten, Kairo, Moschee des Ibn Tulun, Stuck, geschnitten, 9. Jh.
436 Syrien, Keramik, 17. Jh.
437 Persien, Rayy, Keramik, 8. Jh.
438 Persien, Kaschan, Keramik, 13. Jh.

439 Syrie, Damas, mosquée des Omeyyades, marbre incrusté.
440 Tunisie, Kairouan, Grande Mosquée,
plâtre sculpté, XIXᵉ siècle.
441 Tunisie, Tunis, Dar Othman, plâtre
sculpté, XVIIIᵉ siècle.
442 Egypte, Le Caire, palais al-Razzaz, pierre
sculptée, XVᵉ siècle.
443 Maroc, Fès, broderie sur cuir, XIXᵉ
siècle.
444 Espagne, Burgos, plâtre sculpté.

*439 Syria: Damascus, Umayyad Mosque.
Inlaid marble.*
*440 Tunisia: Qairawan, Great Mosque.
Stucco, 19th century.*
*441 Tunisia: Tunis, Dar Othman. Stucco,
18th century.*
*442 Egypt: Cairo, Palace of al-Razziz. Carved
stone, 15th century.*
*443 Morocco: Fez. Embroidery on leather,
19th century.*
444 Spain: Burgos. Stucco.

439 Syrien, Damaskus, Omaijadenmoschee,
Marmor, eingelegt.
440 Tunesien, Kairuan, Große Moschee,
Stuck, geschnitten, 19. Jh.
441 Tunesien, Tunis, Dar Othman, Stuck,
geschnitten, 18. Jh.
442 Ägypten, Kairo, Palast ar-Razzaz, Stein,
behauen, 15. Jh.
443 Marokko, Fez, Stickerei auf Leder,
19. Jh.
444 Spanien, Burgos, Stuck, geschnitten.

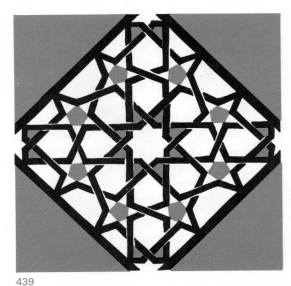
439

440

441

442

443

444

445 Espagne, Grenade, Alhambra, plâtre sculpté, XIVᵉ-XVᵉ siècle.

445 Spain: Granada, Alhambra Palace. Stucco, 14th–15th century.

445 Spanien, Granada, Alhambra, Stuck, geschnitten, 14.–15. Jh.

445

446 Maroc, Fès, peinture sur bois.
447 Maroc, Fès, peinture sur bois.
448 Egypte, Le Caire, musée arabe, bois sculpté, XIIᵉ siècle.
449 Espagne, Grenade, Alhambra, mosaïque de faïence, XIVᵉ siècle.
450 Maroc, Fès, médersa Bou Inaniya, mosaïque de faïence, XIVᵉ siècle.

446 *Morocco: Fez. Painting on wood.*
447 *Morocco: Fez. Painting on wood.*
448 *Egypt: Museum of Islamic Art, Cairo. Carved wood, 12th century.*
449 *Spain: Granada, Alhambra Palace. Tin-glazed earthenware mosaic, 14th century.*
450 *Morocco: Fez. Madrasah of Bu Inaniyya. Tin-glazed earthenware mosaic, 14th century.*

446 Marokko, Fez, Malerei auf Holz.
447 Marokko, Fez, Malerei auf Holz.
448 Ägypten, Kairo, Islamisches Museum, Holz, geschnitzt, 12. Jh.
449 Spanien, Granada, Alhambra, Fayence-mosaik, 14. Jh.
450 Marokko, Fez, Medrese Bu Inaniya, Fayencemosaik, 14. Jh.

446

447

448

449

450

451

452

453

454

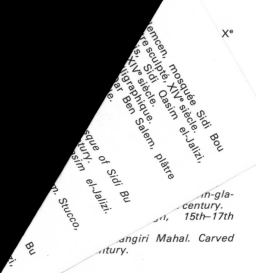

455

456

457

458

459

460

461

Motifs ornementaux végétaux

Une transposition remarquable du réel, conçue dans une géométrie vivante.

Ornamental Plant Motifs

A remarkable transposition of nature, set in an animate geometry

Pflanzliche Ornament-Motive

Eine bemerkenswerte Übertragung der Wirklichkeit, in lebendiger Geometrie entworfen.

461   Maroc, Fès, médersa el-Attarin.

461   Morocco: Fez, Madrasah of al-Attarin.

461   Marokko, Fez, Medrese al-Attarin.

462 Mésopotamie, céramique, IXe siècle.
463 Maroc, Tétouan, bois peint, XIXe siècle.
464 Tunisie, Tunis, musée du Bardo, palais du Bey, carreau de faïence.
465 Perse, céramique, XVIIe siècle.
466 Turquie, céramique, XIXe siècle.

462 *Mesopotamia. Ceramic design, 9th century.*
463 *Morocco: Tetuan. Painted wood, 19th century.*
464 *Tunisia: Bardo Museum, Tunis, Bey Palace. Tin-glazed earthenware tile.*
465 *Iran. Ceramic design, 17th century.*
466 *Turkey. Ceramic design, 19th century.*

462 Mesopotamien, Keramik, 9. Jh.
463 Marokko, Tetuan, Holz, bemalt, 19. Jh.
464 Tunesien, Nationalmuseum im Bardo, Palast des Bey, Fayencefliese.
465 Persien, Keramik, 17. Jh.
466 Türkei, Keramik, 19. Jh.

462

463

464

465

466

467

468

469

470

471 Ornementation arabe.
472 Maroc, plâtre sculpté, XIXᵉ siècle.
473 Egypte, Le Caire, musée arabe, céramique, XIᵉ siècle.
474 Egypte, Le Caire, musée arabe, céramique, XIᵉ siècle.
475 Tunisie, Tunis, musée du Bardo, palais du Bey, carreaux de faïence.

471 *Islamic ornamentation.*
472 *Morocco. Stucco, 19th century.*
473 *Egypt: Museum of Islamic Art, Cairo. Ceramic design, 11th century.*
474 *Egypt: Museum of Islamic Art, Cairo. Ceramic design, 11th century.*
475 *Tunisia: Bardo Museum, Tunis, Bey Palace. Tin-glazed earthenware tiles.*

471 Arabisches Ornament.
472 Marokko, Stuck, geschnitten, 19. Jh.
473 Ägypten, Kairo, Islamisches Museum, Keramik, 11. Jh.
474 Ägypten, Kairo, Islamisches Museum, Keramik, 11. Jh.
475 Tunesien, Nationalmuseum im Bardo, Palast des Bey, Fayencefliesen.

471

472

473

474

475

476

477

478

479

480

481

476 Algérie, Tlemcen, Grande Mosquée, plâtre sculpté, XIIᵉ siècle.
477 Espagne, médina az-Zahara, pierre sculptée, Xᵉ siècle.
478 Espagne, céramique, XVᵉ-XVIIᵉ siècle.
479 Egypte, Le Caire, musée arabe, céramique, XIᵉ siècle.
480 Espagne, Grenade, palais de l'Alhambra, plâtre sculpté, XIIIᵉ-XIVᵉ siècle.
481 Ornementation arabe.

476 *Algeria: Tlemcen, Great Mosque. Stucco, 12th century.*
477 *Spain: Medina al-Zahara. Carved stone, 10th century.*
478 *Spain. Ceramic design, 15th–17th century.*
479 *Egypt: Museum of Islamic Art, Cairo. Ceramic design, 11th century.*
480 *Spain: Granada, Alhambra Palace. Stucco, 13th–14th century.*
481 *Islamic ornamentation.*

476 Algerien, Tlemcen, Große Moschee, Stuck, geschnitten, 12. Jh.
477 Spanien, Medina az-Zahara, Stein, behauen, 10. Jh.
478 Spanien, Keramik, 15.–17. Jh.
479 Ägypten, Kairo, Islamisches Museum, Keramik, 11. Jh.
480 Spanien, Granada, Alhambra, Stuck, geschnitten, 13.–15. Jh.
481 Arabisches Ornament.

482 Tunisie, Kairouan, Grande Mosquée,
plâtre sculpté, IXᵉ siècle.
483 Egypte, Le Caire, musée arabe, bois
sculpté, IXᵉ siècle.
484 Egypte, Le Caire, musée arabe, bois
sculpté, XIIᵉ siècle.
485 Egypte, Le Caire, musée arabe, bois
sculpté, XIIᵉ siècle.

482 *Tunisia: Qairawan, Great Mosque.*
Stucco, 9th century.
483 *Egypt: Museum of Islamic Art, Cairo.*
Carved wood, 9th century.
484 *Egypt: Museum of Islamic Art, Cairo.*
Carved wood, 12th century.
485 *Egypt: Museum of Islamic Art, Cairo.*
Carved wood, 12th century.

482 Tunesien, Kairuan, Große Moschee,
Stuck, geschnitten, 9. Jh.
483 Ägypten, Kairo, Islamisches Museum,
Holz, geschnitzt, 9. Jh.
484 Ägypten, Kairo, Islamisches Museum,
Holz, geschnitzt, 12. Jh.
485 Ägypten, Kairo, Islamisches Museum,
Holz, geschnitzt, 12. Jh.

483

482

484

485

486

487

488

489

490 Turquie, Istanbul, musée Topkapi, cuir brodé, XIXᵉ siècle.
491 Mésopotamie, céramique, IXᵉ siècle.
492 Egypte, Le Caire, musée arabe, bois sculpté, VIIIᵉ siècle.
493 Perse, céramique, VIIIᵉ siècle.
494 Mésopotamie, Raqqa, céramique, XIIᵉ-XIIIᵉ siècle.
495 Iran, céramique, XIIIᵉ siècle.

490 *Turkey: Topkapı Sarayi Museum, Istanbul. Embroidery on leather, 19th century.*
491 *Mesopotamia. Ceramic design, 9th century.*
492 *Egypt: Museum of Islamic Art, Cairo. Carved wood, 8th century.*
493 *Iran. Ceramic design, 8th century.*
494 *Syria: Rakka. Ceramic design, 12th–13th century.*
495 *Iran. Ceramic design, 13th century.*

490 Türkei, Istanbul, Topkapı-Museum, Leder, bestickt, 19. Jh.
491 Mesopotamien, Keramik, 9. Jh.
492 Ägypten, Kairo, Islamisches Museum, Holz, geschnitzt, 8. Jh.
493 Persien, Keramik, 8. Jh.
494 Mesopotamien, Raqqa, Keramik, 12.–13. Jh.
495 Iran, Keramik, 13. Jh.

490

491

492

493

494

495

496

497

498

499

500

496 Turquie, Brousse, Yéchil Tourbé, faïence, XVᵉ siècle.
497 Turquie, Birgi, bois sculpté.
498 Maroc, Fès, médersa Bou Inaniya, plâtre sculpté, XIVᵉ siècle.
499 Perse, céramique, XIIᵉ siècle.
500 Inde, Agra, mausolée d'Itimour ed-Daula, marbre incrusté, XVIIᵉ siècle.

496 *Turkey: Bursa, Green Tomb. Tin-glazed earthenware, 15th century.*
497 *Turkey: Birgi. Carved wood.*
498 *Morocco: Fez, Madrasah of Bu Inaniyya. Stucco, 14th century.*
499 *Iran. Ceramic design, 12th century.*
500 *India: Agra, Mausoleum of Itimad al-Dawla. Inlaid marble, 17th century.*

496 Türkei, Bursa, Grüne Türbe, Fayence, 15. Jh.
497 Türkei, Birgi, Holz, geschnitzt.
498 Marokko, Fez, Medrese Bu Inaniya, Stuck, geschnitten, 14. Jh.
499 Persien, Keramik, 12. Jh.
500 Indien, Agra, Mausoleum des Itimad ud-Daula, Marmor, eingelegt, 17. Jh.

501 Espagne, Saragosse, pierre sculptée, XIᵉ siècle.
502 Algérie, Tlemcen, médersa Sidi Bou Médine, plâtre sculpté, XIVᵉ siècle.
503 Espagne, médina az-Zahara, pierre sculptée, Xᵉ siècle.
504 Espagne, pierre sculptée, Xᵉ siècle.
505 Espagne, pierre sculptée, Xᵉ siècle.

501 *Spain: Saragossa. Carved stone, 11th century.*
502 *Algeria: Tlemcen, Madrasah of Sidi Bu Medina. Stucco, 14th century.*
503 *Spain: Medina al-Zahara. Carved stone, 10th century.*
504 *Spain. Carved stone, 10th century.*
505 *Spain. Carved stone, 10th century.*

501 Spanien, Zaragoza, Stein, behauen, 11. Jh.
502 Algerien, Tlemcen, Medrese von Bu Medine, Stuck, geschnitten, 14. Jh.
503 Spanien, Medina az-Zahara, Stein, behauen, 10. Jh.
504 Spanien, Stein, behauen, 10. Jh.
505 Spanien, Stein, behauen, 10. Jh.

501

502

503

504

505

506

507

508

509

506 Mésopotamie, Raqqa, céramique, XIIe-XIIIe siècle.
507 Algérie, Tlemcen, Grande Mosquée, plâtre sculpté, XIIe siècle.
508 Espagne, médina az-Zahara, pierre sculptée, Xe siècle.
509 Algérie, Tlemcen, Grande Mosquée, plâtre sculpté, XIIe siècle.

506 *Syria: Rakka. Ceramic design, 12th-13th century.*
507 *Algeria: Tlemcen, Great Mosque. Stucco, 12th century.*
508 *Spain: Medina al-Zahara. Carved stone, 10th century.*
509 *Algeria: Tlemcen, Great Mosque. Stucco, 12th century.*

506 Mesopotamien, Raqqa, Keramik, 12.–13. Jh.
507 Algerien, Tlemcen, Große Moschee, Stuck, geschnitten, 12. Jh.
508 Spanien, Medina az-Zahara, Stein, behauen, 10. Jh.
509 Algerien, Tlemcen, Große Moschee, Stuck, geschnitten, 12. Jh.

510 Jérusalem, coupole du Rocher, VIIᵉ-VIIIᵉ
    siècle.
511 Jérusalem, coupole du Rocher, VIIᵉ-VIIIᵉ
    siècle.
512 Egypte, ivoire incrusté, XIIIᵉ siècle.
513 Jérusalem, coupole du Rocher, VIIᵉ-VIIIᵉ
    siècle.
514 Jérusalem, coupole du Rocher, VIIᵉ-VIIIᵉ
    siècle.

510 Jerusalem: Dome of the Rock. 7th–8th
    century.
511 Jerusalem: Dome of the Rock. 7th–8th
    century.
512 Egypt. Inlaid ivory, 13th century.
513 Jerusalem: Dome of the Rock. 7th–8th
    century.
514 Jerusalem: Dome of the Rock. 7th–8th
    century.

510 Jerusalem, Felsendom, 7.–8. Jh.
511 Jerusalem, Felsendom, 7.–8. Jh.
512 Ägypten, Elfenbein, eingelegt, 13. Jh.
513 Jerusalem, Felsendom, 7.–8. Jh.
514 Jerusalem, Felsendom, 7.–8. Jh.

510

511

512

513

514

515

516

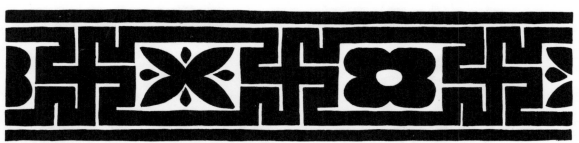

517

518

519

515 Egypte, Le Caire, mosquée Hassan, pierre sculptée, XIVᵉ siècle.
516 Egypte, Le Caire, musée arabe, bois sculpté, VIIᵉ siècle.
517 Turquie, galère impériale, nacre incrustée.
518 Egypte, Le Caire, musée arabe, bois sculpté.
519 Egypte, bibliothèque du Caire, enluminure de Coran, XVᵉ siècle.

515 Egypt: Cairo, Mosque of Sultan Hassan. Carved stone, 14th century.
516 Egypt: Museum of Islamic Art, Cairo. Carved wood, 7th century.
517 Turkey: imperial galley. Inlaid mother-of-pearl.
518 Egypt: Museum of Islamic Art, Cairo. Carved wood.
519 Egypt: National Library, Cairo. Koran illumination, 15th century.

515 Ägypten, Kairo, Moschee des Hassan, Stein, behauen, 14. Jh.
516 Ägypten, Kairo, Islamisches Museum, Holz, geschnitzt, 7. Jh.
517 Türkei, kaiserliche Galeere, Perlmutt, eingelegt.
518 Ägypten, Kairo, Islamisches Museum, Holz, geschnitzt.
519 Ägypten, Bibliothek von Kairo, Miniatur zum Koran, 15. Jh.

520 Perse, céramique, IXᵉ-Xᵉ siècle.
521 Egypte, Le Caire, musée arabe, bois sculpté.
522 Egypte, Le Caire, musée arabe, bois sculpté, XIIᵉ siècle.
523 Egypte, Le Caire, musée arabe, bois sculpté, XIIᵉ siècle.
524 Afghanistan, Ghazni, palais de Massoud III, marbre sculpté, XIIᵉ siècle.
525 Iran, céramique, XIIᵉ siècle.

520 Iran. Ceramic design, 9th–10th century.
521 Egypt: Museum of Islamic Art, Cairo. Carved wood.
522 Egypt: Museum of Islamic Art, Cairo. Carved wood, 12th century.
523 Egypt: Museum of Islamic Art, Cairo. Carved wood, 12th century.
524 Afghanistan: Ghazni, Palace of Massud III. Carved marble, 12th century.
525 Iran. Ceramic design, 12th century.

520 Persien, Keramik, 9.–10. Jh.
521 Ägypten, Kairo, Islamisches Museum, Holz, geschnitzt.
522 Ägypten, Kairo, Islamisches Museum, Holz, geschnitzt, 12. Jh.
523 Ägypten, Kairo, Islamisches Museum, Holz, geschnitzt, 12. Jh.
524 Afghanistan, Ghazna, Palast des Masud III., Marmor, behauen, 12. Jh.
525 Iran, Keramik, 12. Jh.

520

521

522

523

524

525

526

527

528

529

530

531

526 Espagne, médina az-Zahara, pierre sculptée, Xᵉ siècle.
527 Espagne, médina, az-Zahara, pierre sculptée, Xᵉ siècle.
528 Egypte, Le Caire, musée arabe, bois sculptée, XIIᵉ siècle.
529 Egypte, Le Caire, musée arabe, céramique, XIᵉ siècle.
530 Egypte, Le Caire, musée arabe, bois sculpté, IXᵉ siècle.
531 Espagne, médina az-Zahara, pierre sculptée, Xᵉ siècle.

526 *Spain: Medina al-Zahara. Carved stone, 10th century.*
527 *Spain: Medina al-Zahara. Carved stone, 10th century.*
528 *Egypt: Museum of Islamic Art, Cairo. Carved wood, 12th century.*
529 *Egypt: Museum of Islamic Art, Cairo. Ceramic design, 11th century.*
530 *Egypt: Museum of Islamic Art, Cairo. Carved wood, 9th century.*
531 *Spain: Medina al-Zahara. Carved stone, 10th century.*

526 Spanien, Medina az-Zahara, Stein, behauen, 10. Jh.
527 Spanien, Medina az-Zahara, Stein, behauen, 10. Jh.
528 Ägypten, Kairo, Islamisches Museum, Holz, geschnitzt, 12. Jh.
529 Ägypten, Kairo, Islamisches Museum, Keramik, 11. Jh.
530 Ägypten, Kairo, Islamisches Museum, Holz, geschnitzt, 9. Jh.
531 Spanien, Medina az-Zahara, Stein, behauen, 10. Jh.

532 Egypte, Le Caire, musée arabe, bois
    sculpté, XIIᵉ siècle.
533 Egypte, Le Caire, musée arabe, bois
    sculptée, IXᵉ siècle.
534 Egypte, Le Caire, musée arabe, bois
    sculptée, XIIᵉ siècle.
535 Egypte, Le Caire, musée arabe, bois
    sculpté, XIIᵉ siècle.

532 *Egypt: Museum of Islamic Art, Cairo.*
    Carved wood, 12th century.
533 *Egypt: Museum of Islamic Art, Cairo.*
    Carved wood, 9th century.
534 *Egypt: Museum of Islamic Art, Cairo.*
    Carved wood, 12th century.
535 *Egypt: Museum of Islamic Art, Cairo.*
    Carved wood, 12th century.

532 Ägypten, Kairo, Islamisches Museum,
    Holz, geschnitzt, 12. Jh.
533 Ägypten, Kairo, Islamisches Museum,
    Holz, geschnitzt, 9. Jh.
534 Ägypten, Kairo, Islamisches Museum,
    Holz, geschnitzt, 12. Jh.
535 Ägypten, Kairo, Islamisches Museum,
    Holz, geschnitzt, 12. Jh.

532

533

534

535

536 Tunisie, Kairouan, Grande Mosquée, marbre sculpté, IXᵉ siècle.

536 Tunisia: Qairawan, Great Mosque. Carved marble, 9th century.

536 Tunesien, Kairuan, Große Moschee, Marmor, behauen, 9. Jh.

537 Maroc, Fès, mosaïque de faïence, XXᵉ
siècle.
538 Inde, Agra, Tadj Mahall, marbre incrusté, XVIIᵉ siècle.
539 Maroc, Fès, médina el-Bali, plâtre
sculpté.
540 Maroc, Fès, sanctuaire d'Idris II, plâtre
sculpté, XVIIIᵉ siècle.
541 Tunisie, broderie sur cuir, XIXᵉ-XXᵉ
siècle.

*537 Morocco: Fez. Tin-glazed earthenware
mosaic, 20th century.*
*538 India: Agra, Taj Mahal. Inlaid marble,
17th century.*
539 Morocco: Fez, Medina al-Bali. Stucco.
*540 Morocco: Fez, Sanctuary of Idriss II.
Stucco, 18th century.*
*541 Tunisia. Embroidery on leather,
19th–20th century.*

537 Marokko, Fez, Fayencemosaik, 20. Jh.
538 Indien, Agra, Tadsch Mahal, Marmor,
eingelegt, 17. Jh.
539 Marokko, Fez, Medina al-Bali, Stuck,
geschnitten.
540 Marokko, Fez, Mausoleum des Idris II.,
Stuck, geschnitten, 18. Jh.
541 Tunesien, Stickerei auf Leder, 19.–
20. Jh.

537

538

539

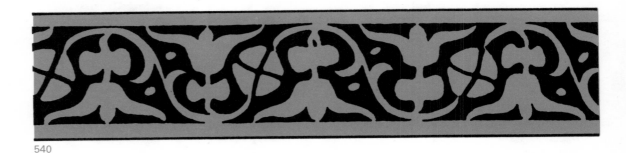

540

541

542

542 Egypte, bibliothèque du Caire, enluminure de Coran, XVe siècle.
543 Egypte, Le Caire, musée arabe, bois
sculpté, XIIe siècle.
544 Turquie, Birgi, mosquée Aydin Oglu
Mehmed Bey, bois sculpté.

542 Egypt: National Library, Cairo. Koran
illumination, 15th century.
543 Egypt: Museum of Islamic Art, Cairo.
Carved wood, 12th century.
544 Turkey: Birgi, Mosque of Aydin Oglu
Mehmed Bey. Carved wood.

542 Ägypten, Bibliothek von Kairo, Miniatur
zum Koran, 15. Jh.
543 Ägypten, Kairo, Islamisches Museum,
Holz, geschnitzt, 12. Jh.
544 Türkei, Birgi, Moschee des Aydın Oğlu
Mehmet Bey, Holz, geschnitzt.

543

544

545 Inde, Agra, Tadj Mahall, marbre incrusté, XVIIᵉ siècle.
546 Inde, Agra, Tadj Mahall, marbre incrusté, XVIIᵉ siècle.
547 Tunisie, Kairouan, marbre sculpté, IXᵉ siècle.
548 Tunisie, Kairouan, marbre sculpté, Xᵉ siècle.

545 *India: Agra, Taj Mahal. Inlaid marble, 17th century.*
546 *India: Agra, Taj Mahal. Inlaid marble, 17th century.*
547 *Tunisia: Qairawan. Carved marble, 9th century.*
548 *Tunisia: Qairawan. Carved marble, 10th century.*

545 Indien, Agra, Tadsch Mahal, Marmor, eingelegt, 17. Jh.
546 Indien, Agra, Tadsch Mahal, Marmor, eingelegt, 17. Jh.
547 Tunesien, Kairuan, Marmor, behauen, 9. Jh.
548 Tunesien, Kairuan, Marmor, behauen, 10. Jh.

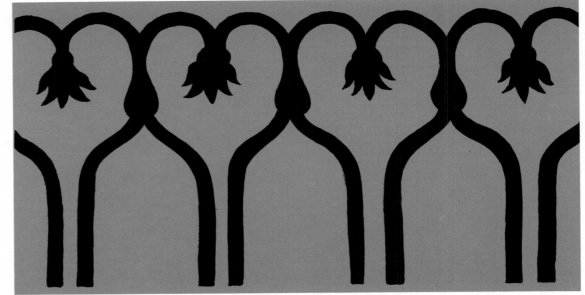

545

546

547

548

549

550

551

552

553 Maroc, Fès, médersa Bou Inaniya, bois
sculpté, XIVᵉ siècle.
554 Espagne, Grenade, Alhambra, plâtre
sculpté, XIVᵉ siècle.
555 Egypte, bibliothèque du Caire, enluminure de Coran, XVᵉ siècle.
556 Ornementation arabe.

553 *Morocco: Fez, Madrasah of Bu Inaniyya.*
Carved wood, 14th century.
554 *Spain: Granada, Alhambra Palace.*
Stucco, 14th century.
555 *Egypt: National Library, Cairo. Koran*
illumination, 15th century.
556 *Islamic ornamentation.*

553 Marokko, Fez, Medrese Bu Inaniya, Holz,
geschnitzt, 14. Jh.
554 Spanien, Granada, Alhambra, Stuck,
geschnitten, 14. Jh.
555 Ägypten, Bibliothek von Kairo, Miniatur
zum Koran, 15. Jh.
556 Arabisches Ornament.

553

554

555

556

557

558

559

560

562

561

557 Turquie, palais de Topkapi, bronze ajouré, XIIIe siècle.
558 Iran, Ispahan, mosquée du Vendredi, mosaïque de faïence, XVe siècle.
559 Espagne, Grenade, palais de l'Alhambra, plâtre sculpté, XIVe siècle.
560 Maroc, Tétouan, bois peint, XIXe siècle.
561 Turquie, ornementation.
562 Turquie, ornementation.

557 *Turkey: Istanbul, Topkapı Palace. Bronze openwork, 13th century.*
558 *Iran: Isfahan, Friday Mosque. Tin-glazed earthenware mosaic, 15th century.*
559 *Spain: Granada, Alhambra Palace. Stucco, 14th century.*
560 *Morocco: Tetuan. Painted wood, 19th century.*
561 *Turkey. Ornamentation.*
562 *Turkey. Ornamentation.*

557 Türkei, Istanbul, Topkapı-Palast, Bronze, durchbrochen gearbeitet, 13. Jh.
558 Iran, Isfahan, Freitagsmoschee, Fayencemosaik, 15. Jh.
559 Spanien, Granada, Alhambra, Stuck, geschnitten, 14. Jh.
560 Marokko, Tetuan, Holz, bemalt, 19. Jh.
561 Türkei, Ornament.
562 Türkei, Ornament.

563 Espagne, médina az-Zahara, marbre sculpté, Xᵉ siècle.
564 Espagne, Grenade, palais de l'Alhambra, plâtre sculpté, XIVᵉ-XVᵉ siècle.
565 Tunisie, Kairouan, plâtre sculpté, XIXᵉ-XXᵉ siècle.
566 Egypte, bronze, XIIIᵉ-XIVᵉ siècle.

563 *Spain: Medina al-Zahara. Carved marble, 10th century.*
564 *Spain: Granada, Alhambra Palace. Stucco, 14th–15th century.*
565 *Tunisia: Qairawan. Stucco, 19th–20th century.*
566 *Egypt. Bronzework, 13th–14th century.*

563 Spanien, Medina az-Zahara, Marmor, behauen, 10. Jh.
564 Spanien, Granada, Alhambra, Stuck, geschnitten, 14.–15. Jh.
565 Tunesien, Kairuan, Stuck, geschnitten, 19.–20. Jh.
566 Ägypten, Bronze, 13.–14. Jh.

563

564

565

566

567

568

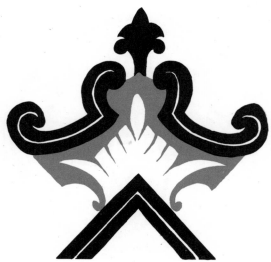

569

570

571

572 Turquie, céramique, XVIIe siècle.
573 Turquie, brique vernie, XVIe-XVIIe siècle.
574 Tunisie, Kairouan, Grande Mosquée, pierre sculptée, IXe siècle.
575 Maroc, Marrakech, musée Dar Si Saïd, céramique.
576 Turquie, céramique, XVIe siècle.
577 Tunisie, Kairouan, pierre sculptée, IXe siècle.

572 Turkey. Ceramic design, 17th century.
573 Turkey. Glazed brick, 16th–17th century.
574 Tunisia: Qairawan, Great Mosque. Carved stone, 9th century.
575 Morocco: Dar si Said Museum, Marrakesh. Ceramic design.
576 Turkey. Ceramic design, 16th century.
577 Tunisia: Qairawan. Carved stone, 9th century.

572 Türkei, Keramik, 17. Jh.
573 Türkei, Ziegel, glasiert, 16.–17. Jh.
574 Tunesien, Kairuan, Große Moschee, Stein, behauen, 9. Jh.
575 Marokko, Marrakesch, Museum Dar Si Said, Keramik.
576 Türkei, Keramik, 16. Jh.
577 Tunesien, Kairuan, Stein, behauen, 9. Jh.

572

573

574

575

576

577

578

579

580

581

578 Turquie, céramique, XVIe-XVIIe siècle.
579 Maroc, Fès, céramique.
580 Maroc, Fès, mosaïque de faïence, XXe siècle.
581 Tunisie, Kairouan, marbre sculpté, IXe siècle.

578 Turkey. Ceramic design, 16th–17th century.
579 Morocco: Fez. Ceramic design.
580 Morocco: Fez. Tin-glazed earthenware mosaic, 20th century.
581 Tunisia: Qairawan. Carved marble, 9th century.

578 Türkei, Keramik, 16.–17. Jh.
579 Marokko, Fez, Keramik.
580 Marokko, Fez, Fayencemosaik, 20. Jh.
581 Tunesien, Kairuan, Marmor, behauen, 9. Jh.

582　　　583　　　584

585

586

587

588

589

590

591

592

593

594 Maroc, Fès, médersa el-Attarin, mosaïque de faïence, XIV° siècle.
595 Turquie, Brousse, porte du Yéchil Djami,
bois sculpté, XV° siècle.
596 Turquie, Istanbul, mosquée Zal Mahmoud Pacha, peinture, XVI° siècle.
597 Algérie, broderie sur velours.
598 Egypte, ivoire sculpté, XIII° siècle.

*594 Morocco: Fez, Madrasah of al-Attarin.
Tin-glazed earthenware mosaic, 14th
century.*
*595 Turkey: Bursa, gate of the Green Mos-
que. Carved wood, 15th century.*
*596 Turkey: Istanbul, Mosque of Zal Mah-
mud Pasha. Painting, 16th century.*
597 Algeria. Embroidery on velvet.
598 Egypt. Carved ivory, 13th century.

594 Marokko, Fez, Medrese al-Attarin,
Fayencemosaik, 14. Jh.
595 Türkei, Bursa, Portal der Grünen
Moschee, Holz, geschnitzt, 15. Jh.
596 Türkei, Istanbul, Moschee des Zal Mah-
mut Pascha, Malerei, 16. Jh.
597 Algerien, Stickerei auf Samt.
598 Ägypten, Elfenbein, geschnitzt, 13. Jh.

594

595

596

597

598

599

599 Syrie, Damas, hôpital al-Qaymari, plâtre sculpté, XIIIᵉ siècle.

599 *Syria: Damascus, al-Qaymari Hospital. Stucco, 13th century.*

599 Syrien, Damaskus, Spital al-Qaymari, Stuck, geschnitten, 13. Jh.

600

601

602

603

604

605

606

607

608 Turquie, céramique, XVIIᵉ siècle.
609 Maroc, Fès, médersa el-Attarin, marbre sculpté, XIVᵉ siècle.
610 Algérie, Tlemcen, mosquée Sidi Haloui, plâtre sculpté, XIVᵉ siècle.
611 Egypte, Le Caire, mosquée Ibn Touloun, plâtre sculpté, IXᵉ siècle.
612 Egypte, Le Caire, mosquée el-Azhar, plâtre sculpté.

608 Turkey. Ceramic design, 17th century.
609 Morocco: Fez, Madrasah of al-Attarin. Carved marble, 14th century.
610 Algeria: Tlemcen, Mosque of Sidi Lahloui. Stucco, 14th century.
611 Egypt: Cairo, Mosque of Ibn Tulun. Stucco, 9th century.
612 Egypt: Cairo, Mosque of al-Azhar. Stucco.

608 Türkei, Keramik, 17. Jh.
609 Marokko, Fez, Medrese al-Attarin, Marmor, behauen, 14. Jh.
610 Algerien, Tlemcen, Moschee des Sidi 'l-Halwi, Stuck, geschnitten, 14. Jh.
611 Ägypten, Kairo, Moschee des Ibn Tulun, Stuck, geschnitten, 9. Jh.
612 Ägypten, Kairo, Moschee al-Azhar, Stuck, geschnitten.

608

609

610

611

612

613

614

615

616

613 Maroc, Fès, médersa Bou Inaniya, plâtre sculpté, XIVᵉ siècle.
614 Perse, céramique, VIIᵉ siècle.
615 Algérie, Tlemcen, mosquée Sidi Bel Hassen, plâtre sculpté, XIIIᵉ siècle.
616 Maroc, Rabat, porte des Oudaïa, pierre sculptée, XIIᵉ siècle.

613 Morocco: Fez, Madrasah of Bu Inaniyya. Stucco, 14th century.
614 Iran. Ceramic design, 7th century.
615 Algeria: Tlemcen, Mosque of Sidi Bel Hassan. Stucco, 13th century.
616 Morocco: Rabat, Oudaia Gate. Carved stone, 12th century.

613 Marokko, Fez, Medrese Bu Inaniya, Stuck, geschnitten, 14. Jh.
614 Persien, Keramik, 7. Jh.
615 Algerien, Tlemcen, Moschee des Sidi Bel Hassen, Stuck, geschnitten, 13. Jh.
616 Marokko, Rabat, Tor der Oudaias, Stein, behauen, 12. Jh.

617 Algérie, Tlemcen, mosquée Sidi Bel
       Hassen, plâtre sculpté, XIVᵉ siècle.
618 Algérie, Tlemcen, mosquée Sidi Bou
       Médine, plâtre sculpté, XIVᵉ siècle.
619 Algérie, Tlemcen, mosquée Sidi Bou
       Médine, plâtre sculpté, XIVᵉ siècle.

617 *Algeria: Tlemcen, Mosque of Sidi Bel
       Hassan. Stucco, 14th century.*
618 *Algeria: Tlemcen, Mosque of Sidi Bu
       Medina. Stucco, 14th century.*
619 *Algeria: Tlemcen, Mosque of Sidi Bu
       Medina. Stucco, 14th century.*

617 Algerien, Tlemcen, Moschee des Sidi
       Bel Hassen, Stuck, geschnitten, 14. Jh.
618 Algerien, Tlemcen, Moschee von Bu
       Medine, Stuck, geschnitten, 14. Jh.
619 Algerien, Tlemcen, Moschee von Bu
       Medine, Stuck, geschnitten, 14. Jh.

617

618

619

620

620   Algérie, Tlemcen, mosquée Oulad el-
Iman, plâtre sculpté XIVᵉ siècle.

*620   Algeria: Tlemcen, Mosque of Ulad al-
Iman. Stucco, 14th century.*

620   Algerien, Tlemcen, Moschee Ulad al-
Iman, Stuck, geschnitten, 14. Jh.

621 Espagne, pierre sculptée, Xe siècle.
622 Espagne, pierre sculptée, Xe siècle.
623 Maroc, plâtre sculpté, XIXe siècle.

621 Spain. Carved stone. 10th century.
622 Spain. Carved stone. 10th century.
623 Morocco. Stucco, 19th century.

621 Spanien, Stein, behauen, 10. Jh.
622 Spanien, Stein, behauen, 10. Jh.
623 Marokko, Stuck, geschnitten, 19. Jh.

621

622

623

624

625

626

627

628 Egypte, Le Caire, musée arabe, bois sculpté.
629 Maroc, Tétouan, bois peint, XVIII° siècle.
630 Maroc, Marrakech, musée Dar Si Saïd, céramique.
631 Maroc, plâtre sculpté, XIX° siècle.
632 Egypte, Le Caire, mosquée Hassan, marbre sculpté, XIV° siècle.
633 Egypte, Le Caire, musée arabe, bois sculpté, VIII° siècle.

628 Egypt: Museum of Islamic Art, Cairo. Carved wood.
629 Morocco: Tetuan. Painted wood, 18th century.
630 Morocco: Dar si Said Museum, Marrakesh. Ceramic design.
631 Morocco. Stucco, 19th century.
632 Egypt: Cairo, Mosque of Sultan Hassan. Carved marble, 14th century.
633 Egypt: Egyptian Museum, Cairo. Carved wood, 8th century.

628 Ägypten, Kairo, Islamisches Museum, Holz, geschnitzt
629 Marokko, Tetuan, Holz, bemalt, 18. Jh.
630 Marokko, Marrakesch, Museum Dar Si Said, Keramik.
631 Marokko, Stuck, geschnitten, 19. Jh.
632 Ägypten, Kairo, Moschee des Hassan, Marmor, behauen, 14. Jh.
633 Ägypten, Kairo, Islamisches Museum, Holz, geschnitzt, 8. Jh.

628

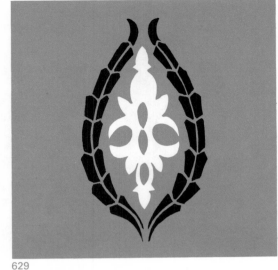

629

630

631

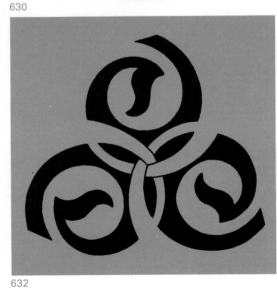

632

633

634

635

636

637 Iran, céramique, XIVᵉ-XVᵉ siècle.
638 Tunisie, Kairouan, Grande Mosquée,
céramique, IXᵉ siècle.
639 Maroc, Fès, étoffe, XIXᵉ siècle.
640 Tunisie, Kairouan, Grande Mosquée,
céramique, IXᵉ siècle.
641 Tunisie, Tunis, musée du Bardo, palais
du Bey, carreau de faïence.

637 Iran. Ceramic design, 14th–15th century.
638 Tunisia: Qairawan, Great Mosque.
Ceramic design, 9th century.
639 Morocco: Fez. Fabric, 19th century.
640 Tunisia: Qairawan, Great Mosque.
Ceramic design, 9th century.
641 Tunisia: Bardo Museum, Tunis, Bey
Palace. Tin-glazed earthenware tile.

637 Iran, Keramik, 14.–15. Jh.
638 Tunesien, Kairuan, Große Moschee,
Keramik, 9. Jh.
639 Marokko, Fez, Stoff, 9. Jh.
640 Tunesien, Kairuan, Große Moschee,
Keramik, 9. Jh.
641 Tunesien, Nationalmuseum im Bardo,
Palast des Bey, Fayencefliese

637

638

639

640

641

642

643

644

645

646 Egypte, Le Caire, mosquée el-Hakim, plâtre sculpté, Xe siècle.
647 Transoxiane, Samarkand, céramique, VIIIe-IXe siècle.
648 Egypte, Le Caire, musée arabe, bois sculpté, XIe siècle.
649 Egypte, Le Caire, musée arabe, bois sculpté, XIe siècle.

646 *Egypt: Cairo, Mosque of al-Hakim. Stucco, 10th century.*
647 *Transoxiana: Samarkand. Ceramic design, 8th–9th century.*
648 *Egypt: Museum of Islamic Art, Cairo. Carved wood, 11th century.*
649 *Egypt: Museum of Islamic Art, Cairo. Carved wood, 11th century.*

646 Ägypten, Kairo, Moschee al-Hakim, Stuck, geschnitten, 10. Jh.
647 Usbekische SSR, Sowjetunion, bis 16. Jh. Transoxanien, Samarkand, Keramik, 8.–9. Jh.
648 Ägypten, Kairo, Islamisches Museum, Holz, geschnitzt, 11. Jh.
649 Ägypten, Kairo, Islamisches Museum, Holz, geschnitzt, 11. Jh.

646

647

648

649

650

651

652

653 Espagne, Grenade, palais de l'Alhambra, plâtre sculpté, XIIIᵉ-XIVᵉ siècle.
654 Espagne, Grenade, palais de l'Alhambra, plâtre sculpté, XIIIᵉ-XIVᵉ siècle.
655 Egypte, Le Caire, musée arabe, bois sculpté, IXᵉ siècle.
656 Egypte, Le Caire, musée arabe, bois sculpté.

653 *Spain: Granada, Alhambra Palace. Stucco, 13th–14th century.*
654 *Spain: Granada, Alhambra Palace. Stucco, 13th–14th century.*
655 *Egypt: Museum of Islamic Art, Cairo. Carved wood, 9th century.*
656 *Egypt: Museum of Islamic Art, Cairo. Carved wood.*

653 Spanien, Granada, Alhambra, Stuck, geschnitten, 13.–14. Jh.
654 Spanien, Granada, Alhambra, Stuck, geschnitten, 13.–14. Jh.
655 Ägypten, Kairo, Islamisches Museum, Holz, geschnitten, 9. Jh.
656 Ägypten, Kairo, Islamisches Museum, Holz, geschnitzt.

653

654

655

656

657

658

659

657 Tunisie, Kairouan, Grande Mosquée, marbre sculpté, IXᵉ siècle.
658 Tunisie, Kairouan, marbre sculpté, IXᵉ siècle.
659 Tunisie, Kairouan, bois peint, IXᵉ siècle.
660 Egypte, Le Caire, musée arabe, bois sculpté.

657 *Tunisia: Qairawan, Great Mosque. Carved marble, 9th century.*
658 *Tunisia: Qairawan. Carved marble, 9th century.*
659 *Tunisia: Qairawan. Painted wood, 9th century.*
660 *Egypt: Museum of Islamic Art, Cairo. Carved wood.*

657 Tunesien, Kairuan, Große Moschee, Marmor, behauen, 9. Jh.
658 Tunesien, Kairuan, Marmor, behauen, 9. Jh.
659 Tunesien, Kairuan, Holz, bemalt, 9. Jh.
660 Ägypten, Kairo, Islamisches Museum, Holz, geschnitzt.

660

661 Egypte, Le Caire, mu_____ ___ bois sculpté.
662 Afghanistan, Ghazni, palais de Massoud III, marbre sculpté, XIIᵉ siècle.
663 Algérie, Qal'a des Beni Hammad, pierre sculptée, Xᵉ-XIᵉ siècle.
664 Tunisie, Kairouan, Grande Mosquée, bois peint, IXᵉ siècle.
665 Tunisie, Kairouan, Grande Mosquée, bois peint, IXᵉ siècle.

661 *Egypt: Museum of Islamic Art, Cairo. Carved wood.*
662 *Afghanistan: Ghazni, Palace of Massud III. Carved marble, 12th century.*
663 *Algeria: Beni Hammad Qala. Carved stone, 10th–11th century.*
664 *Tunisia: Qairawan, Great Mosque. Painted wood, 9th century.*
665 *Tunisia: Qairawan, Great Mosque. Painted wood, 9th century.*

661 Ägypten, Kairo, Islamisches Museum, Holz, geschnitzt.
662 Afghanistan, Ghazna, Palast des Masud III., Marmor, behauen, 12. Jh.
663 Algerien, Qalaa der Banu Hammad, Stein, behauen, 10.–11. Jh.
664 Tunesien, Kairuan, Große Moschee, Holz, bemalt, 9. Jh.
665 Tunesien, Kairuan, Große Moschee, Holz, bemalt, 9. Jh.

661

662

663

664

665

666

667

668

669

666 Egypte, Le Caire, musée arabe, bois sculpté, XIe siècle.
667 Egypte, bibliothèque du Caire, enluminure de Coran, XVe siècle.
668 Tunisie, Kairouan, Grande Mosquée, bois peint, IXe siècle.
669 Tunisie, Kairouan, Grande Mosquée, bois peint, IXe siècle.

666 Egypt: Museum of Islamic Art, Cairo. Carved wood, 11th century.
667 Egypt: National Library, Cairo. Koran illumination, 15th century.
668 Tunisia: Qairawan, Great Mosque. Painted wood, 9th century.
669 Tunisia: Qairawan, Great Mosque. Painted wood, 9th century.

666 Ägypten, Kairo, Islamisches Museum, Holz, geschnitzt, 11. Jh.
667 Ägypten, Bibliothek von Kairo, Miniatur zum Koran, 15. Jh.
668 Tunesien, Kairuan, Große Moschee, Holz, bemalt, 9. Jh.
669 Tunesien, Kairuan, Große Moschee, Holz, bemalt, 9. Jh.

670

671

672

673

674

675

676

677

678

679

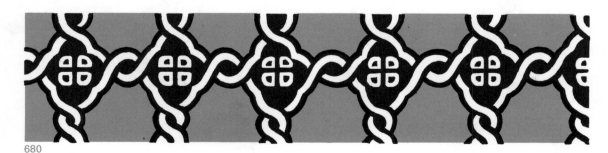

680

676 Syrie, Damas, céramique, XVᵉ siècle.
677 Tunisie, Sfax, Grande Mosquée, pierre sculptée Xᵉ siècle.
678 Maroc, Tétouan, bois peint, XIXᵉ siècle.
679 Maroc, Marrakech, mausolée Saadien, XVIᵉ-XVIIᵉ siècle.
680 Tunisie, Kairouan, Grande Mosquée, bois peint, XIᵉ siècle.

676 *Syria: Damascus. Ceramic design, 15th century.*
677 *Tunisia: Sfax, Great Mosque. Carved stone, 10th century.*
678 *Morocco: Tetuan. Painted wood, 19th century.*
679 *Morocco: Marrakesh, Sadi Mausoleum. 16th–17th century.*
680 *Tunisia: Qairawan, Great Mosque. Painted wood, 11th century.*

676 Syrien, Damaskus, Keramik, 15. Jh.
677 Tunesien, Sfax, Große Moschee, Stein, behauen, 10. Jh.
678 Marokko, Tetuan, Holz, bemalt, 19. Jh.
679 Marokko, Marrakesch, Saadiermausoleum, 16.–17. Jh.
680 Tunesien, Kairuan, Große Moschee, Holz, bemalt, 11. Jh.

681 Turquie, Brousse, faïence.
682 Algérie, Tlemcen, mosquée Sidi Bou
 Médine, décors peints, XVIIIᵉ siècle.
683 Turquie, ornementation.
684 Turquie, musée Topkapi, broderie, XVIIIᵉ
 siècle.
685 Turquie, céramique, XVIᵉ siècle.

681 Turkey: Bursa. Tin-glazed earthenware.
682 Algeria: Tlemcen, Mosque of Sidi Bu
 Medina. Painted decorations, 18th
 century.
683 Turkey. Ornamentation.
684 Turkey: Topkapı Sarayi Museum, Istanbul. Embroidery, 18th century.
685 Turkey. Ceramic design, 16th century.

681 Türkei, Bursa, Fayence.
682 Algerien, Tlemcen, Moschee von Bu
 Medine, bemalte Verzierungen, 18. Jh.
683 Türkei, Ornament.
684 Türkei, Istanbul, Topkapı-Museum,
 Stickerei, 18. Jh.
685 Türkei, Keramik, 16. Jh.

681

682

683

684

685

686

Motifs ornementaux floraux

Plein de bouquets,
de fraîcheur et de parfums.

Ornamental Floral Motifs

A world of fresh and
fragrant posies

Florale Ornament-Motive

Voller Sträuße, Frische und Duft.

686 Tunisie, Gabès, médersa Mouradiya,
plâtre sculpté, XVIIᵉ siècle.

*686 Tunisia: Gabès, Mouradiya Madrasah.
Stucco, 17th century.*

686 Tunesien, Gabes, Medrese Muradiya,
Stuck, geschnitten, 17. Jh.

687 Maroc, Marrakech, palais de la Bahia, bois peint, XIXᵉ siècle.
688 Tunisie, broderie sur velours, XXᵉ siècle.
689 Maroc, Marrakech, palais de la Bahia, bois peint, XIXᵉ siècle.
690 Maroc, Marrakech, palais de la Bahia, bois peint, XIXᵉ siècle.
691 Tunisie, broderie sur cuir, XIXᵉ-XXᵉ siècle.
692 Maroc, Fès, broderie, XIXᵉ siècle.

687 *Morocco: Marrakesh, Bahia Palace. Painted wood, 19th century.*
688 *Tunisia. Embroidery on velvet, 20th century.*
689 *Morocco: Marrakesh, Bahia Palace. Painted wood, 19th century.*
690 *Morocco: Marrakesh, Bahia Palace. Painted wood, 19th century.*
691 *Tunisia. Embroidery on leather, 19th–20th century.*
692 *Morocco: Fez. Embroidery, 19th century.*

687 Marokko, Marrakesch, Bahia-Palast, Holz, bemalt, 19. Jh.
688 Tunesien, Stickerei auf Samt, 20. Jh.
689 Marokko, Marrakesch, Bahia-Palast, Holz, bemalt, 19. Jh.
690 Marokko, Marrakesch, Bahia-Palast, Holz, bemalt, 19. Jh.
691 Tunesien, Stickerei auf Leder, 19.–20. Jh.
692 Marokko, Fez, Stickerei, 19. Jh.

687

688

689

690

691

692

693

694

695

696

697

698

699

700

701

702

703

704

705

706

707

708

709 Syrie, Damas, plaque de faïence d'influence chinoise, XVᵉ siècle.
710 Perse, Erdine, céramique, XVᵉ siècle.
711 Perse, céramique, XVIIᵉ siècle.
712 Syrie, Damas, plaque de faïence d'influence chinoise, XVᵉ siècle.
713 Syrie, Damas, plaque de faïence d'influence chinoise, XVᵉ siècle.

709 Syria: Damascus. Tin-glazed earthenware panel, Chinese influence, 15th century.
710 Iran: Erdine. Ceramic design, 15th century.
711 Iran. Ceramic design, 17th century.
712 Syria: Damascus. Tin-glazed earthenware panel, Chinese influence, 15th century.
713 Syria: Damascus. Tin-glazed earthenware panel, Chinese influence, 15th century.

709 Syrien, Damaskus, Fayencefliese mit chinesischem Einfluß, 15. Jh.
710 Persien, Erdine, Keramik, 15. Jh.
711 Persien, Keramik, 17. Jh.
712 Syrien, Damaskus, Fayencefliese mit chinesischem Einfluß, 15. Jh.
713 Syrien, Damaskus, Fayencefliese mit chinesischem Einfluß, 15. Jh.

709

710

711

712

713

714

715

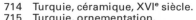

714 Turquie, céramique, XVIᵉ siècle.
715 Turquie, ornementation.
716 Tunisie, Tunis, Dar Djellouli, carreau de faïence, XVIIIᵉ siècle.
717 Maroc, Marrakech, palais de la Bahia, bois peint, XIXᵉ siècle.
718 Turquie, Iznik, céramique, XVᵉ siècle.

714 Turkey. Ceramic design, 16th century.
715 Turkey. Ornamentation.
716 Tunisia: Tunis, Dar Djellouli. Tin-glazed earthenware tile, 18th century.
717 Morocco: Marrakesh, Bahia Palace. Painted wood, 19th century.
718 Turkey: Iznik. Ceramic design, 15th century.

714 Türkei, Keramik, 16. Jh.
715 Türkei, Ornament.
716 Tunesien, Tunis, Dar Djelluli, Fayencefliese, 18. Jh.
717 Marokko, Marrakesch, Bahia-Palast, Holz, bemalt, 19. Jh.
718 Türkei, Iznik, Keramik, 15. Jh.

716

717

718

719

720

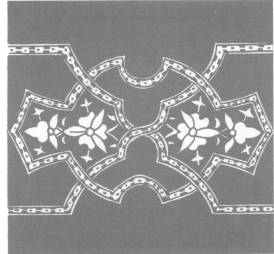

721

722

723

724

725

726

727

728

729

730

731

732

733

734

735

736

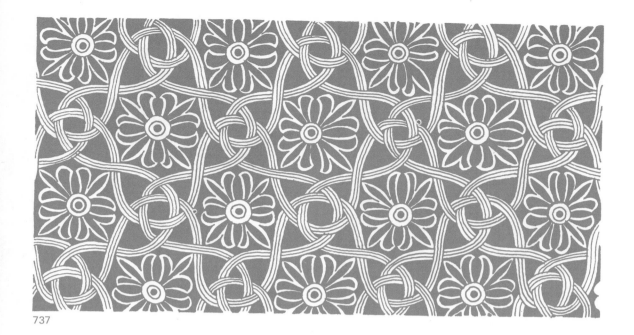

737

738

739

740

741 Tunisie, broderie sur cuir, XIXᵉ-XXᵉ
    siècle.
742 Tunisie, broderie sur cuir, XXᵉ siècle.
743 Turquie, Iznik, céramique, XVIᵉ siècle.
744 Tunisie, carreau de faïence.
745 Tunisie, broderie sur cuir, XXᵉ siècle.

*741 Tunisia. Embroidery on leather, 19th–
    20th century.*
*742 Tunisia. Embroidery on leather, 20th
    century.*
*743 Turkey: Iznik. Ceramic design, 16th cen-
    tury.*
744 Tunisia. Tin-glazed earthenware tile.
*745 Tunisia. Embroidery on leather, 20th
    century.*

741 Tunesien, Stickerei auf Leder, 19.–
    20. Jh.
742 Tunesien, Stickerei auf Leder, 20. Jh.
743 Türkei, Iznik, Keramik, 16. Jh.
744 Tunesien, Fayencefliese.
745 Tunesien, Stickerei auf Leder, 20. Jh.

741

742

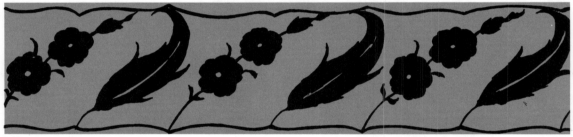

743

744

745

746

747

748

749

746 Maroc, étoffe, XIXᵉ siècle.
747 Maroc, étoffe, XVIIᵉ siècle.
748 Maroc, soie brochée, XIXᵉ siècle.
749 Egypte ou Syrie, Le Caire, musée arabe, bois sculpté, VIIIᵉ siècle.
750 Tunisie, Tunis, Dar Khalsi, carreau de faïence, XVIIIᵉ siècle.
751 Turquie, plaque de faïence, XVIᵉ-XVIIᵉ siècle.
752 Turquie, ornementation.

746 *Morocco. Fabric, 19th century.*
747 *Morocco. Fabric, 17th century.*
748 *Morocco. Silk brocade, 19th century.*
749 *Egypt or Syria: Museum of Islamic Art, Cairo. Carved wood, 8th century.*
750 *Tunisia: Tunis, Dar Khalsi. Tin-glazed earthenware tile, 18th century.*
751 *Turkey. Tin-glazed earthenware panel, 16th–17th century.*
752 *Turkey. Ornamentation.*

746 Marokko, Stoff, 19. Jh.
747 Marokko, Stoff, 17. Jh.
748 Marokko, Seide, durchwirkt, 19. Jh.
749 Ägypten oder Syrien, Kairo, Islamisches Museum, Holz, geschnitzt, 8. Jh.
750 Tunesien, Tunis, Dar Khalsi, Fayencefliese, 18. Jh.
751 Türkei, Fayencefliese, 16.–17. Jh.
752 Türkei, Ornament.

750

751

752

753

754

755

756

757

758

759

760

761

762

763

764

765

766

767

768

769

 770
 771
 772
 773

 774
 775
 776
 777

 778
 779
 780
 781

 782
 783
 784
 785

 786
 787
 788
 789

770 Maroc, Fès, étoffe.
771 Inde, Agra, mausolée d'Itimour ed-Daula, marbre incrusté, XVIIᵉ siècle.
772 Turquie, Istanbul, musée des Faïences, faïence, XVIIᵉ siècle.
773 Tunisie, Kairouan, Grande Mosquée, céramique, IXᵉ siècle.
774 Turquie, céramique, XVIᵉ siècle.
775 Turquie, brique vernie, XVIᵉ-XVIIᵉ siècle.
776 Maroc, Fès, broderie, XIXᵉ siècle.
777 Perse, céramique, XVIᵉ siècle.
778 Egypte, bibliothèque du Caire, enluminure de Coran, XVᵉ siècle.
779 Tunisie, Tunis, musée du Bardo, palais du Bey, carreau de faïence.
780 Syrie, Alep, bois peint, XVIIᵉ siècle.
781 Tunisie, carreau de faïence.
782 Turquie, ornementation.
783 Tunisie, Tunis, Dar el-Haddad, bois peint, XVIIIᵉ siècle.
784 Turquie, faïence.
785 Tunisie, Tunis, Dar el-Haddad, bois peint, XVIIIᵉ siècle.

770 *Morocco: Fez. Fabric.*
771 *India: Agra, Mausoleum of Itimad al-Dawla. Inlaid marble, 17th century.*
772 *Turkey: Museum of Turkish and Islamic Art, Istanbul. Tin-glazed earthenware, 17th century.*
773 *Tunisia: Qairawan, Great Mosque. Ceramic design, 9th century.*
774 *Turkey. Ceramic design, 16th century.*
775 *Turkey. Glazed brick, 16th–17th century.*
776 *Morocco: Fez. Embroidery, 19th century.*
777 *Iran. Ceramic design, 16th century.*
778 *Egypt: National Library, Cairo. Koran illumination, 15th century.*
779 *Tunisia: Bardo Museum, Tunis. Tin-glazed earthenware tile.*
780 *Syria: Aleppo. Painted wood, 17th century.*
781 *Tunisia. Tin-glazed earthenware tile.*
782 *Turkey. Ornamentation.*
783 *Tunisia: Tunis, Dar el-Haddad. Painted wood, 18th century.*
784 *Turkey. Tin-glazed earthenware.*
785 *Tunisia: Tunis, Dar el-Haddad. Painted wood, 18th century.*

770 Marokko, Fez, Stoff.
771 Indien, Agra, Mausoleum des Itimad ud-Daula, Marmor, eingelegt, 17. Jh.
772 Türkei, Istanbul, Fayence-Museum, Fayence, 17. Jh.
773 Tunesien, Kairuan, Große Moschee, Keramik, 9. Jh.
774 Türkei, Keramik, 16. Jh.
775 Türkei, Ziegel, glasiert 16.–17. Jh.
776 Marokko, Fez, Stickerei, 19. Jh.
777 Persien, Keramik, 16. Jh.
778 Ägypten, Bibliothek von Kairo, Miniatur zum Koran, 15. Jh.
779 Tunesien, Nationalmuseum im Bardo, Fayencefliese.
780 Syrien, Aleppo, Holz, bemalt, 17. Jh.
781 Tunesien, Fayencefliese.
782 Türkei, Ornament.
783 Tunesien, Tunis, Dar al-Haddad, Holz, bemalt, 18. Jh.
784 Türkei, Fayence.
785 Tunesien, Tunis, Dar al-Haddad, Holz, bemalt, 18. Jh.

790

791

792

793

794

795

796

797

798

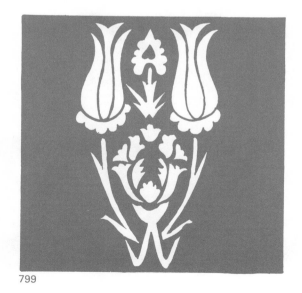

799

800 Turquie, ornementation.
801 Syrie, brique vernie, XIVᵉ siècle.
802 Syrie, brique vernie, XIVᵉ siècle.
803 Syrie, Damas, musée national, salle damascène, bois sculpté et peint, XVIIIᵉ siècle.

800 Turkey. Ornamentation.
801 Syria. Glazed brick, 14th century.
802 Syria. Glazed brick, 14th century.
803 Syria: National Museum, Damascus, Damascan Room. Carved and painted wood, 18th century.

800 Türkei, Ornament.
801 Syrien, Ziegel, glasiert, 14. Jh.
802 Syrien, Ziegel, glasiert, 14. Jh.
803 Syrien, Damaskus, Nationalmuseum, Damaszenersaal, Holz, geschnitzt und bemalt, 18. Jh.

800

801

802

803

804

805

806

807

808 Turquie, Istanbul, musée Topkapi, ivoire incrusté.
809 Turquie, galère impériale, nacre incrustée.
810 Turquie, galère impériale, nacre incrustée.
811 Turquie, galère impériale, nacre incrustée.

808 Turkey: Topkapı Sarayi Museum, Istanbul. Inlaid ivory.
809 Turkey: imperial galley. Inlaid mother-of-pearl.
810 Turkey: imperial galley. Inlaid mother-of-pearl.
811 Turkey: imperial galley. Inlaid mother-of-pearl.

808 Türkei, Istanbul, Topkapı-Museum, Elfenbein, eingelegt.
809 Türkei, kaiserliche Galeere, Perlmutt, eingelegt.
810 Türkei, kaiserliche Galeere, Perlmutt, eingelegt.
811 Türkei, kaiserliche Galeere, Perlmutt, eingelegt.

808

809

810

811

812

813

814

815

816

812 Maroc, Meknès, maison Ben Azzouz, plâtre sculpté, XVe-XVIe siècle.
813 Turquie, galère impériale, nacre incrustée.
814 Syrie, Damas, musée national, salle damascène, bois sculpté et peint, XVIIIe siècle.
815 Turquie, broderie, XVIIIe siècle.
816 Perse, Kirman, céramique, XVIIe siècle.

812 *Morocco: Meknès, Ben Azzouz House. Stucco, 15th–16th century.*
813 *Turkey: imperial galley. Inlaid mother-of-pearl.*
814 *Syria: National Museum, Damascus, Damascan Room. Carved and painted wood, 18th century.*
815 *Turkey. Embroidery, 18th century.*
816 *Iran: Kerman. Ceramic design, 17th century.*

812 Marokko, Meknes, Haus Ben Azzuz, Stuck, geschnitten, 15.–16. Jh.
813 Türkei, kaiserliche Galeere, Perlmutt, eingelegt.
814 Syrien, Damaskus, Nationalmuseum, Damaszenersaal, Holz, geschnitzt und bemalt, 18. Jh.
815 Türkei, Stickerei, 18. Jh.
816 Persien, Kerman, Keramik, 17. Jh.

817 Turquie, Iznik, céramique, XVIᵉ siècle.
818 Turquie, Istanbul, musée Topkapi, broderie.
819 Turquie, Iznik, céramique, XVIᵉ siècle.
820 Turquie, Iznik, céramique, XVIᵉ siècle.
821 Turquie, musée Topkapi, enluminure sur cuir, XVIIᵉ siècle.
822 Syrie, Alep, bois peint, XVIIᵉ siècle.
823 Tunisie, Tunis, Dar Djellouli, carreau de faïence, XVIIIᵉ siècle.
824 Maroc, carreau de faïence, façon espagnole, XVIIᵉ siècle.
825 Maroc, carreau de faïence, façon espagnole, XVIIᵉ siècle.
826 Tunisie, Tunis, Dar Bel Khoja, carreaux de faïence, XVIIIᵉ siècle.
827 Tunisie, Tunis, Dar Khalsi, carreau de faïence, XVIIIᵉ siècle.
828 Iran, Ispahan, mosquée du Shah, céramique, XVIIᵉ siècle.

817 *Turkey: Iznik. Ceramic design, 16th century.*
818 *Turkey: Topkapı Sarayi Museum, Istanbul. Embroidery.*
819 *Turkey: Iznik. Ceramic design, 16th century.*
820 *Turkey: Iznik. Ceramic design, 16th century.*
821 *Turkey: Topkapı Sarayi Museum, Istanbul. Painting on leather, 17th century.*
822 *Syria: Aleppo. Painted wood, 17th century.*
823 *Tunisia: Tunis, Dar Djellouli. Tin-glazed earthenware tile, 18th century.*
824 *Morocco. Tin-glazed earthenware tile in Spanish style, 17th century.*
825 *Morocco. Tin-glazed earthenware tile in Spanish style, 17th century.*
826 *Tunisia: Tunis, Dar Bel Khoja. Tin-glazed earthenware tiles, 18th century.*
827 *Tunisia: Tunis, Dar Khalsi. Tin-glazed earthenware tile, 18th century.*
828 *Iran: Isfahan, Mosque of the Shah. Ceramic design, 17th century.*

817 Türkei, Iznik, Keramik, 16. Jh.
818 Türkei, Istanbul, Topkapı-Museum, Stickerei.
819 Türkei, Iznik, Keramik, 16. Jh.
820 Türkei, Iznik, Keramik, 16. Jh.
821 Türkei, Istanbul, Topkapı-Museum, Miniatur auf Leder, 17. Jh.
822 Syrien, Aleppo, Holz, bemalt, 17. Jh.
823 Tunesien, Tunis, Dar Djelluli, Fayencefliese, 18. Jh.
824 Marokko, Fayencefliese nach spanischer Art, 17. Jh.
825 Marokko, Fayencefliese nach spanischer Art, 17. Jh.
826 Tunesien, Tunis, Dar Bel Khoja, Fayencefliesen, 18. Jh.
827 Tunesien, Tunis, Dar Khalsi, Fayencefliese, 18. Jh.
828 Iran, Isfahan, Schahmoschee, Keramik, 17. Jh.

817

818

819

820

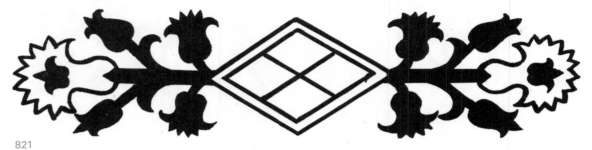
821

822

823

824

825

826

827

828

829

830

829 Turquie, Brousse, céramique, XVIe siècle.
830 Turquie, Brousse, céramique, XVIe siècle.
831 Turquie, ornementation.

829 Turkey: Bursa. Ceramic design, 16th century.
830 Turkey: Bursa. Ceramic design, 16th century.
831 Turkey. Ornamentation.

829 Türkei, Bursa, Keramik, 16. Jh.
830 Türkei, Bursa, Keramik, 16. Jh.
831 Türkei, Ornament.

831

832 Turquie, Istanbul, musée Topkapi,
étoffe, XVIIᵉ siècle.
833 Turquie, velours de Scutari, XVIᵉ siècle.
834 Turquie, plâtre sculpté, XXᵉ siècle.
835 Turquie, ornementation.

832 Turkey: Topkapı Sarayi Museum, Istanbul. Fabric, 17th century.
833 Turkey. Skutari velvet, 16th century.
834 Turkey. Stucco, 20th century.
835 Turkey. Ornamentation.

832 Türkei, Istanbul, Topkapı-Museum, Stoff, 17. Jh.
833 Türkei, Samt von Skutari, 16. Jh.
834 Türkei, Stuck, geschnitten, 20. Jh.
835 Türkei, Ornament.

832

833

834

835

836

837

838

839

840

842

841

843

844

845

Motifs ornementaux définis par une forme enveloppante
Ornements
le plus souvent ornementés

Enclosed Ornamental Motifs
Ornaments that are highly
ornamented themselves

Durch umschließende Form bestimmte Ornament-Motive
Ornament an sich,
meist selbst noch verziert.

846 Egypte, Le Caire, mosquée el-Azhar,
bois sculpté.

846 *Egypt: Cairo, Mosque of al-Azhar.
Carved wood.*

846 Ägypten, Kairo, Moschee al-Azhar, Holz,
geschnitzt.

847

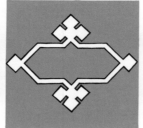
848

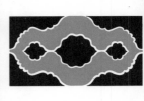
849

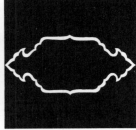
850

851

852

853

854

855

856

857

858

859

860

861

862

863

864

865

866

867

868

869

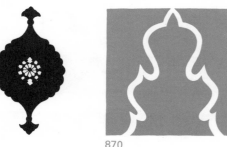

870

871

872

873

874

875

876

877

878

879

880

881

865 Algérie, Tlemcen, mosquée Sidi Bou Médine, plâtre sculpté, XIVᵉ siècle.
866 Tunisie, Tunis, musée du Bardo, palais du Bey, carreau de faïence.
867 Algérie, Tlemcen, mosquée Sidi Bel Hassen, plâtre sculpté, XIIIᵉ siècle.
868 Iran, Ispahan, mosquée du Shah, mosaïque de faïence, XVIIᵉ siècle.
869 Iran, Ispahan, mosquée de la mère du Shah, mosaïque de faïence, XVIIIᵉ siècle.
870 Egypte, Le Caire, musée arabe, bois sculpté, XIIᵉ siècle.
871 Enluminure de Coran.
872 Maroc, Tétouan, bois peint, XIXᵉ siècle.
873 Tunisie, Tunis, Dar Mamoghli, décor clouté, XVIIᵉ siècle.
874 Tunisie, Tunis, Dar Mamoghli, décor clouté, XVIIIᵉ siècle.
875 Turquie, nacre incrustée, XVIIᵉ siècle.
876 Turquie, céramique, XVIᵉ siècle.
877 Turquie, Divrighi, Grande Mosquée, pierre sculptée, XIIIᵉ siècle.

865 Algeria: Tlemcen, Mosque of Sidi Bu Medina. Stucco, 14th century.
866 Tunisia: Bardo Museum, Tunis. Tin-glazed earthenware tile.
867 Algeria: Tlemcen, Mosque of Sidi Bel Hassan. Stucco, 13th century.
868 Iran: Isfahan, Mosque of the Shah. Tin-glazed earthenware mosaic, 17th century.
869 Iran: Isfahan, Mosque of the Shah's Mother. Tin-glazed earthenware mosaic, 18th century.
870 Egypt: Museum of Islamic Art, Cairo, Carved wood, 12th century.
871 Koran illumination.
872 Morocco: Tetuan. Painted wood, 19th century.
873 Tunisia: Tunis, Dar Mamoghli. Studwork, 18th century.
874 Tunisia: Tunis, Dar Mamoghli. Studwork, 18th century.
875 Turkey. Inlaid mother-of-pearl, 17th century.
876 Turkey. Ceramic design, 16th century.
877 Turkey: Divriği, Great Mosque. Carved stone, 13th century.

865 Algerien, Tlemcen, Moschee von Bu Medine, Stuck, geschnitten, 14. Jh.
866 Tunesien, Nationalmuseum im Bardo, Fayencefliese.
867 Algerien, Tlemcen, Moschee des Sidi Bel Hassen, Stuck, geschnitten, 13. Jh.
868 Iran, Isfahan, Schahmoschee, Fayence-mosaik, 17. Jh.
869 Iran, Isfahan, Moschee der Schahmutter, Fayencemosaik, 18. Jh.
870 Ägypten, Kairo, Islamisches Museum, Holz, geschnitzt, 12. Jh.
871 Miniatur zum Koran.
872 Marokko, Tetuan, Holz, bemalt, 19. Jh.
873 Tunesien, Tunis, Dar Mamoghli, Beschlagdekor, 18. Jh.
874 Tunesien, Tunis, Dar Mamoghli, Beschlagdekor, 18. Jh.
875 Türkei, Perlmutt, eingelegt, 17. Jh.
876 Türkei, Keramik, 16. Jh.
877 Türkei, Divriği, Große Moschee, Stein, behauen, 13. Jh.

878 Turquie, bronze, XVIe siècle.
879 Turquie, céramique, XVIe siècle.
880 Egypte, Le Caire, musée arabe, bois sculpté, XIIe siècle.
881 Turquie, Brousse, Yéchil Tourbé, faïence, XVe siècle.
882 Tunisie, broderie sur cuir.
883 Maroc, Fès, broderie, XVIIIe siècle.
884 Egypte, Le Caire, musée arabe, bois sculpté, IXe siècle.
885 Egypte, Le Caire, mosquée Ibn Touloun, bois sculpté, VIIIe-IXe siècle.
886 Maroc, Fès, broderie, XIXe siècle.

878 Turkey. Bronzework, 16th century.
879 Turkey. Ceramic design, 16th century.
880 Egypt: Museum of Islamic Art, Cairo. Carved wood, 12th century.
881 Turkey: Bursa, Green Tomb. Tin-glazed earthenware, 15th century.
882 Tunisia. Embroidery on leather.
883 Morocco: Fez. Embroidery, 18th century.
884 Egypt: Museum of Islamic Art, Cairo. Carved wood, 9th century.
885 Egypt: Cairo, Mosque of Ibn Tulun. Carved wood, 8th–9th century.
886 Morocco: Fez. Embroidery, 19th century.

878 Türkei, Bronze, 16. Jh.
879 Türkei, Keramik, 16. Jh.
880 Ägypten, Kairo, Islamisches Museum, Holz, geschnitzt, 12. Jh.
881 Türkei, Bursa, Grüne Türbe, Fayence, 15. Jh.
882 Tunesien, Stickerei auf Leder.
883 Marokko, Fez, Stickerei, 18. Jh.
884 Ägypten, Kairo, Islamisches Museum, Holz, geschnitzt, 9. Jh.
885 Ägypten, Kairo, Moschee des Ibn Tulun, Holz, geschnitzt, 8.–9. Jh.
886 Marokko, Fez, Stickerei, 19. Jh.

882

883

884

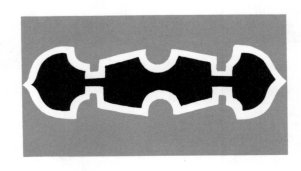

885

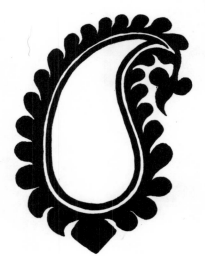

886

887

888

889

887 Iran, Tabriz, mosquée Bleue, mosaïque de faïence, XVe siècle.
888 Turquie, Brousse, Yéchil Djami, bois peint, XVe siècle.
889 Tunisie, Tunis, Dar Zaouche, carreaux de faïence, XIXe siècle.
890 Maroc, enluminure de Coran, XVIe siècle.

887 *Iran: Tabriz, Blue Mosque. Tin-glazed earthenware mosaic, 15th century.*
888 *Turkey: Bursa, Green Mosque. Painted wood, 15th century.*
889 *Tunisia: Tunis, Dar Zaouche. Tin-glazed earthenware tiles, 19th century.*
890 *Morocco. Koran illumination, 16th century.*

887 Iran, Täbriz, Blaue Moschee, Fayence-mosaik, 15. Jh.
888 Türkei, Bursa, Grüne Moschee, Holz, bemalt, 15. Jh.
889 Tunesien, Tunis, Dar Zausche, Fayence-fliesen, 19. Jh.
890 Marokko, Miniatur zum Koran, 16. Jh.

890

891 Syrie, Damas, composition calligraphique, XXᵉ siècle.
892 Maroc, Tanger, cuir incrusté d'or.
893 Algérie, Tlemcen, mosquée de Sidi
Brahim, plâtre sculpté, XIVᵉ siècle.
894 Turquie, ornementation.
895 Algérie, Tlemcen, mosquée Sidi Bou
Médine, plâtre sculpté, XIVᵉ siècle.
896 Iran, Ispahan, mosquée du Vendredi,
mosaïque de faïence, XVᵉ siècle.

891 Syria: Damascus. Calligraphy, 20th cen-
tury.
892 Morocco: Tangier. Leather inlaid with
gold.
893 Algeria: Tlemcen, Mosque of Sidi
Brahim. Stucco, 14th century.
894 Turkey. Ornamentation.
895 Algeria: Tlemcen, Mosque of Sidi Bu
Medina. Stucco, 14th century.
896 Iran: Isfahan, Friday Mosque. Tin-glazed
earthenware mosaic, 15th century.

891 Syrien, Damaskus, kalligraphischer
Schriftdekor, 20. Jh.
892 Marokko, Tanger, Leder, mit Gold eingelegt.
893 Algerien, Tlemcen, Moschee des Sidi
Brahim, Stuck, geschnitten, 14. Jh.
894 Türkei, Ornament.
895 Algerien, Tlemcen, Moschee von Bu
Medine, Stuck, geschnitten, 14. Jh.
896 Iran, Isfahan, Freitagsmoschee,
Fayencemosaik, 15. Jh.

891

892

893

894

895

896

897

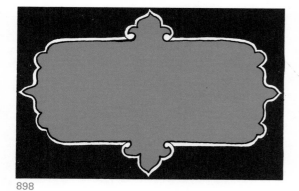

898

899

900

901

902 Tunisie, peinture sous verre, monture
fabuleuse du Prophète, XXᵉ siècle.
903 Perse, brique vernie, XVᵉ siècle.
904 Composition calligraphique turque en
forme de cigogne, XIIIᵉ siècle.

902 *Tunisia. Painting under glass, legendary
mount of the Prophet Muhammad, 20th
century.*
903 *Iran. Glazed brick, 15th century.*
904 *Turkish calligraphic design in the shape
of a stork, 13th century.*

902 Tunesien, Hinterglasmalerei, legendäres
Reittier des Propheten, 20. Jh.
903 Persien, Ziegel, glasiert, 15. Jh.
904 Türkischer kalligraphischer Schriftdekor
in Gestalt eines Storches, 13. Jh.

902

903

904

Motifs ornementaux comportant une forme humaine ou animale

Inattendus, prohibés
par le Prophète,
et pourtant parfois présents.

Human and Animal Ornamental Motifs

Despite the Prophet's ban,
they make an occasional
unexpected appearance.

Ornament-Motive mit Menschen- oder Tiergestalten

Manchmal vorhanden,
ganz unerwartet,
trotz Verbot des Propheten.

905

905 Mésopotamie, Samarra, peinture murale, IXᵉ siècle.

905 Iraq: Samarra, Wall painting, 9th century.

905 Mesopotamien, Samarra, Wandmalerei, 9. Jh.

906 Italie du Sud, ivoire sculpté, XIᵉ siècle.
907 Tunisie, broderie.
908 Tunisie, broderie.
909 Italie du Sud, ivoire sculpté, XIᵉ siècle.
910 Italie du Sud, ivoire sculpté, XIᵉ siècle.

906 *Southern Italy. Carved ivory, 11th century.*
907 *Tunisia. Embroidery.*
908 *Tunisia. Embroidery.*
909 *Southern Italy. Carved ivory, 11th century.*
910 *Southern Italy. Carved ivory, 11th century.*

906 Süditalien, Elfenbein, geschnitzt, 11. Jh.
907 Tunesien, Stickerei.
908 Tunesien, Stickerei.
909 Süditalien, Elfenbein, geschnitzt, 11. Jh.
910 Süditalien, Elfenbein, geschnitzt, 11. Jh.

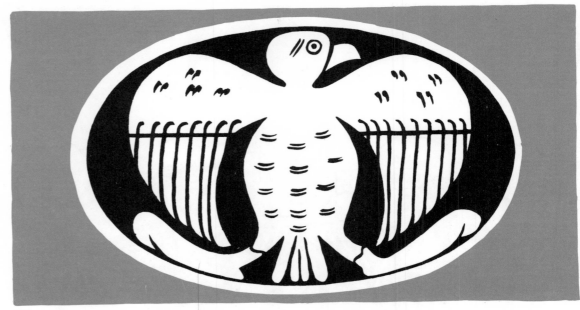

906

907

908

909

910

911

912

913

914

915 Espagne, ivoire sculpté, Xᵉ-XIᵉ siècle.
916 Espagne, ivoire sculpté, Xᵉ-XIᵉ siècle.
917 Italie du Sud, ivoire sculpté, XIᵉ siècle.
918 Italie du Sud, ivoire sculpté, XIᵉ siècle.
919 Espagne, Burgos, plâtre sculpté.
920 Espagne, ivoire sculpté, Xᵉ-XIᵉ siècle.

915 *Spain. Carved ivory, 10th–11th century.*
916 *Spain. Carved ivory, 10th–11th century.*
917 *Southern Italy. Carved ivory, 11th century.*
918 *Southern Italy. Carved ivory, 11th century.*
919 *Spain: Burgos. Stucco.*
920 *Spain. Carved ivory, 10th–11th century.*

915 Spanien, Elfenbein, geschnitzt, 10.–11. Jh.
916 Spanien, Elfenbein, geschnitzt, 10.–11. Jh.
917 Süditalien, Elfenbein, geschnitzt, 11. Jh.
918 Süditalien, Elfenbein, geschnitzt, 11. Jh.
919 Spanien, Burgos, Stuck, geschnitten.
920 Spanien, Elfenbein, geschnitzt, 10.–11. Jh.

915

916

917

918

919

920

921

922

924

925

921 Perse, Hamadan, pierre sculptée, Xᵉ-XIIᵉ siècle.
922 Syrie, Alep, bois peint, XVIIIᵉ siècle.
923 Tunisie, broderie.
924 Egypte, Le Caire, musée arabe, filtre de gargoulette, terre cuite.
925 Mésopotamie, verre peint, XIIᵉ siècle.

921 Iran: Hamadan. Carved stone, 10th–12th century.
922 Syria: Aleppo. Painted wood, 18th century.
923 Tunisia. Embroidery.
924 Egypt: Museum of Islamic Art, Cairo. Water-cooler filter, terracotta.
925 Mesopotamia. Painted glass, 12th century.

921 Persien, Hamadan, Stein, behauen, 10.-12. Jh.
922 Syrien, Aleppo, Holz, bemalt, 18. Jh.
923 Tunesien, Stickerei.
924 Ägypten, Kairo, Islamisches Museum, Filter eines Wasserkruges, Irdenware.
925 Mesopotamien, Glas, bemalt, 12. Jh.

926 Tunisie, broderie.
927 Calligraphie arabe, lettre.
928 Perse, brique vernie, XVᵉ siècle.
929 Mésopotamie, céramique, IXᵉ-Xᵉ siècle.
930 Tunisie, Nabeul, céramique.

926 Tunisia. Embroidery.
927 Arabic character.
928 Iran. Glazed brick, 15th century.
929 Mesopotamia. Ceramic design, 9th–10th century.
930 Tunisia: Nabeul. Ceramic design.

926 Tunesien, Stickerei.
927 Arabische Kalligraphie, Buchstabe.
928 Persien, Ziegel, glasiert, 15. Jh.
929 Mesopotamien, Keramik, 9.–10. Jh.
930 Tunesien, Nabeul, Keramik.

926

927

928

929

930

931

932

933

934

935

936

931 Tunisie, Tunis, musée du Bardo, palais du Bey, céramique.
932 Mésopotamie, Raqqa, céramique, X^e-XIe siècle.
933 Perse, céramique, VIIIe-IXe siècle.
934 Tunisie, broderie.
935 Iran, céramique, X^e-XIe siècle.
936 Tunisie, céramique.

931 *Tunisia: Bardo Museum, Tunis. Ceramic design.*
932 *Syria: Rakka. Ceramic design, 10th–11th century.*
933 *Iran. Ceramic design, 8th–9th century.*
934 *Tunisia. Embroidery.*
935 *Iran. Ceramic design, 10th–11th century.*
936 *Tunisia. Ceramic design.*

931 Tunesien, Nationalmuseum im Bardo, Keramik.
932 Mesopotamien, Raqqa, Keramik, 10.–11. Jh.
933 Persien, Keramik, 8.–9. Jh.
934 Tunesien, Stickerei.
935 Iran, Keramik, 10.–11. Jh.
936 Tunesien, Keramik.

937 Syrie, faïence, XIVe siècle.
938 Iran, céramique, Xe-XIe siècle.
939 Italie du Sud, ivoire sculpté, XIe siècle.
940 Turquie, broderie.
941 Iran, céramique, Xe-XIe siècle.
942 Perse, céramique, VIIIe siècle.

937 Syria. Tin-glazed earthenware, 14th century.
938 Iran. Ceramic design, 10th–11th century.
939 Southern Italy. Carved ivory, 11th century.
940 Turkey. Embroidery.
941 Iran. Ceramic design, 10th–11th century.
942 Iran. Ceramic design, 8th century.

937 Syrien, Fayence, 14. Jh.
938 Iran, Keramik, 10.–11. Jh.
939 Süditalien, Elfenbein, geschnitzt, 11. Jh.
940 Türkei, Stickerei.
941 Iran, Keramik, 10.–11. Jh.
942 Persien, Keramik, 8. Jh.

937

938

939

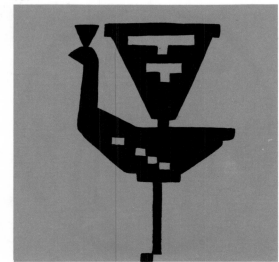

940

941

942

943

944

943 Sicile ou Espagne, étoffe, XIᵉ-XIIᵉ siècle.
944 Etoffe, XIᵉ siècle.

943 Sicily or Spain. Fabric, 11th–12th century.
944 Fabric, 11th century.

943 Sizilien oder Spanien, Stoff, 11.–12. Jh.
944 Stoff, 11. Jh.

945

946

947

948

949

950

951

952

953

954

955

956

957

958

959

960

961

962

963

964

965

966

967

968

969

970

971

972

973

974

975

976

977

978 Turquie, Iznik, céramique, XVIe siècle.
979 Iran, céramique, XVIIe siècle.
980 Sicile, Palerme, bois peint, XIIe siècle.
981 Perse, céramique, XIIIe siècle.
982 Perse, céramique, VIIIe siècle.
983 Italie du Sud, ivoire sculpté, XIe siècle.

978 *Turkey: Iznik. Ceramic design, 16th century.*
979 *Iran. Ceramic design, 17th century.*
980 *Sicily: Palermo. Painted wood, 12th century.*
981 *Iran. Ceramic design, 13th century.*
982 *Iran. Ceramic design, 8th century.*
983 *Southern Italy. Carved ivory, 11th century.*

978 Türkei, Iznik, Keramik, 16. Jh.
979 Iran, Keramik, 17. Jh.
980 Sizilien, Palermo, Holz, bemalt, 12. Jh.
981 Persien, Keramik, 13. Jh.
982 Persien, Keramik, 8. Jh.
983 Süditalien, Elfenbein, geschnitzt, 11. Jh.

978

979

980

981

982

983

984

985

984 Sicile, ivoire sculpté, XIIIᵉ siècle.
985 Sicile, ivoire, sculpté, XIIIᵉ siècle.
986 Egypte, Le Caire, musée arabe, bois sculpté, VIIᵉ siècle.

984 Sicily. Carved ivory, 13th century.
985 Sicily. Carved ivory, 13th century.
986 Egypt: Museum of Islamic Art, Cairo. Carved wood, 7th century.

984 Sizilien, Elfenbein, geschnitzt, 13. Jh.
985 Sizilien, Elfenbein, geschnitzt, 13. Jh.
986 Ägypten, Kairo, Islamisches Museum, Holz, geschnitzt, 7. Jh.

986

987 Turquie, Iznik, céramique, XVe siècle.
988 Egypte, Nuremberg, Germanisches Nationalmuseum, étoffe, XIe siècle.
989 Italie du Sud, ivoire sculpté, XIe siècle.
990 Italie du Sud, ivoire sculpté, XIe siècle.
991 Egypte, Le Caire, musée arabe, bois sculpté, IXe-Xe siècle.
992 Perse ou Irak septentrional, bronze, XIIe-XIIIe siècle.

987 Turkey: Iznik. Ceramic design, 16th century.
988 Egypt: Germanisches Nationalmuseum, Nuremburg. Fabric, 11th century.
989 Southern Italy. Carved ivory, 11th century.
990 Southern Italy. Carved ivory, 11th century.
991 Egypt: Egyptian Museum, Cairo. Carved wood, 9th–10th century.
992 Iran or Iraq. Bronzework, 12th–13th century.

987 Türkei, Iznik, Keramik, 16. Jh.
988 Ägypten, Nürnberg, Germanisches Nationalmuseum, Stoff, 11. Jh.
989 Süditalien, Elfenbein, geschnitzt, 11. Jh.
990 Süditalien, Elfenbein, geschnitzt, 11. Jh.
991 Ägypten, Kairo, Islamisches Museum, Holz, geschnitzt, 9.–10. Jh.
992 Persien oder Irak, Bronze, 12.–13. Jh.

987

988

989

990

991

992

993

994

993 Mésopotamie, Raqqa, céramique, Xe-XIe siècle.
994 Egypte, Le Caire, musée arabe, bois sculpté, XIe siècle.
995 Syrie, Qasr al-Hair al-Garbi, pierre sculptée, VIIIe siècle.

993 Syria: Rakka. Ceramic design, 10th–11th century.
994 Egypt: Museum of Islamic Art, Cairo. Carved wood, 11th century.
995 Syria: Qasr al-hair al-Gharbi. Carved stone, 8th century.

993 Mesopotamien, Raqqa, Keramik, 10.–11. Jh.
994 Ägypten, Kairo, Islamisches Museum, Holz, geschnitzt, 11. Jh.
995 Syrien, Qasr al-Hair al-Gharbi, Stein, behauen, 8. Jh.

995

996 Italie du Sud, ivoire sculpté, XIe siècle.
997 Perse, Rai, céramique, VIIIe siècle.
998 Calligraphie pictographique, portrait d'Ali, gendre du Prophète.
999 Maroc, Fès, étoffe, XIXe siècle.

996 Southern Italy. Carved ivory, 11th century.
997 Iran: Rayy. Ceramic design, 8th century.
998 Pictographic calligraphy: portrait of Ali, son-in-law of the Prophet Muhammad.
999 Morocco: Fez. Fabric, 19th century.

996 Süditalien, Elfenbein, geschnitzt, 11. Jh.
997 Persien, Rayy, Keramik, 8. Jh.
998 Figürliche Kalligraphie, Porträt Alis, des Schwiegersohnes des Propheten.
999 Marokko, Fez, Stoff, 19. Jh.

996

997

998

999

1000

TURQUIE

77, 78, 87, 158, 159, 235, 237, 255, 260, 268, 298, 332, 335, 336, 358, 360, 379, 395, 497, 517, 544, 561, 562, 582, 583, 584, 588, 589, 590, 593, 603, 643, 681, 683, 693, 694, 695, 696, 697, 698, 702, 703, 706, 707, 715, 719, 731, 752, 757, 760, 761, 782, 784, 788, 790, 794, 798, 800, 808, 809, 810, 811, 813, 818, 831, 835, 849, 850, 853, 860, 877, 894, 940, 962

XIIIᵉ siècle: 426, 557

XVᵉ siècle: 170, 195, 261, 458, 496, 595, 718, 740, 804, 841, 861, 881, 888

XVIᵉ siècle: 171, 205, 258, 300, 455, 576, 596, 636, 670, 685, 699, 700, 708, 714, 724, 729, 734, 735, 743, 768, 774, 797, 799, 817, 819, 820, 829, 830, 833, 840, 845, 847, 859, 864, 876, 878, 879, 899, 978, 987

XVIᵉ-XVIIᵉ siècle: 573, 578, 751, 758, 775, 789

XVIIᵉ siècle: 457, 572, 608, 723, 766, 772, 786, 821, 854, 875, 920

XVIIIᵉ siècle: 684, 701, 705, 722, 815

XIXᵉ siècle: 466, 490, 733

XXᵉ siècle: 834

584, 588, 589, 590, 593, 643, 681, 683, 693, 694, 695, 696, 697, 698, 702, 703, 706, 707, 715, 719, 731, 752, 757, 760, 761, 782, 784, 788, 790, 794, 798, 800, 808, 809, 810, 811, 813, 818, 831, 835, 849, 850, 853, 860, 894, 940, 962

13th century: 426, 557, 603, 877

15th century: 170, 195, 261, 458, 496, 595, 718, 740, 804, 841, 861, 881, 888

16th century: 171, 205, 258, 300, 455, 576, 596, 636, 670, 685, 699, 700, 708, 714, 724, 729, 734, 735, 743, 754, 768, 774, 797, 799, 817, 819, 820, 829, 830, 833, 840, 845, 847, 859, 864, 876, 878, 879, 899, 978, 987

16th–17th century: 573, 578, 751, 758, 775, 789

17th century: 457, 572, 608, 723, 766, 772, 786, 821, 832, 854, 875

18th century: 684, 701, 705, 722, 748

19th century: 466, 490, 733

20th century: 834

808, 809, 810, 811, 813, 818, 831, 835, 849, 850, 853, 860, 894, 940, 962

13. Jh.: 426, 557, 603, 877

15. Jh.: 170, 195, 261, 458, 496, 595, 718, 740, 804, 841, 861, 881, 888

16. Jh.: 171, 205, 258, 300, 455, 576, 596, 636, 670, 685, 699, 700, 708, 714, 724, 729, 734, 735, 743, 768, 774, 797, 799, 817, 819, 820, 829, 830, 833, 840, 845, 847, 859, 864, 876, 878, 879, 899, 978, 987

16.–17. Jh.: 573, 578, 751, 758, 775, 789

17. Jh.: 457, 572, 608, 723, 766, 772, 786, 821, 854, 875, 920

18. Jh.: 684, 701, 705, 722, 815

19. Jh.: 466, 490, 733

20. Jh.: 834

USBEKISCHE SSR, Sowjetunion, bis 16. Jh. Transoxanien

8.–9. Jh.: 248, 276, 277, 642, 647

10. Jh.: 456, 469

1001   Calligraphie arabe, lettre.

1001   Arabic character.

1001   Arabische Kalligraphie, Buchstabe.